STUDIES IN VAIṢṆAVISM AND TĀNTRICISM

STUDIES IN VAIṢṆAVISM AND TĀNTRICISM

(Revised and Enlarged Edition)

By

M.N. SIRCAR

BHARATIYA KALA PRAKASHAN
DELHI-INDIA

Published by :
C.P. Gautam
Bharatiya Kala Prakashan
3421-A, IInd Floor., Narang Colony,
Tri Nagar, Delhi-110035
Ph. 7153083

Edition : 2000

ISBN : 81-86050-54-X

Laser Typesetting by :
A-One Graphics
X-4, Gali No. 2, Brahmpuri,
Delhi-110053, Ph. : 2183470

Printed at :
Santosh Offset Press
Delhi-110035

Foreword

It is perilous thing for a non-specialist to write on so formidable a subject as philosophy anything whatsoever, even a foreword, involving as it does, comprehensive knowledge of the topic and other qualifications. Yet I have been asked to do it, a request I cannot refuse. Dr. M.N. Sircar is a philosopher of international reputation who has made his mark by his solid contributions to philosophy and religion and this the latest product of his fecund pen does ample justice to him both by its depth of matter and lucidity of manner. It is a helpful and useful book on Hindu Mysticism in the most comprehensive sense of the term, giving us wealth of information, subtle, appropriate and suggestive criticism and a constructive approach to one of the most fundamental problems of human though in an original manner. The boo! is dwelling at great length upon Vaiṣṇavism in its mysticaı aspect and Tāntricism from the same angle of vision. The book contains nineteen chapters each of which may be regarded as a single unit being devoted to a single topic. In a dramatic manner, as it were, the first chapter entitled "Reason, Revelation and Faith" conducts us into the very heart of the subject by demonstrating the futility of reason as an instru-ment of discovering the ultimate Truth, by assessing the value of revelation and last of all by giving us the true significance of faith. Here we get in a short compass an evalution of philosophy and religion or more properly the philosophy of Religion by a writer who himself might be regarded as a philosophical mystic of the truest type. We are told at the outset "Religion is not reflection on life. It is the sympathetic understanding of life. It is living experience. It is direct contact with the living Reality." This by no means is to be discovered by reason; it is to be discovered by faith and faith alone, for as the author observes, "Reflection leaves us cold, indifferent and cannot give the joyousness of spirit. It can only give us the intellectual chart of spiritual life, which affords at best the foundation of faith in the light of reason." In the second chapter "Contemplation and Rapport," we are shown that the way of the mystic is superior to that of the philosopher. The philosopher is primarily a man of emotion and intution. The author very significantly puts the difference in a pointed way when he says, "The contemplation of values is a matter of transcendent reflection but rapport is the actual identification with the divine spirit with all its creative expression." Step by step the author leads us to his principal topic Vāiṣṇavism which is a typical example of aesthetic dynamism, a veritable kingdom of spirit in which "Will" becomes the spontaneous expression of bliss. The third chapter "Philosophical Mysticism" goes deep into the complexities of the subject and gives us a critical estimate of Vaiṣṇavism as philosophical mysticism of the transcendental type. In Vaiṣṇavism we get the symphony of the whole rather that the music of the parts. It engrosses the seeking soul. The reader can get the whole of Vaiṣṇavism in its mystical aspect in the concluding words of the author towards the end of the Chapter. "Naturally philosophic mysticism in Vaiṣṇavism is not the sense of exhaltation or rapport because of a sudden movement and expression in spirit in its superior height. It is the calm delight which flows from quiet repose of being necessary to enjoy the concrete expression of spirit in its integral setting. It is the opening of consciousness in wideness and vastness. Vaiṣṇavism does not seek annihilation or the denial of life but the breaking down of the barriers which constitute separate existence."

The integral realisation denies separation and presents the Reality in its full setting, in its essence and in its glories. In the fifth chapter "Ethical and Moral Mysticism" the author dwells further on the topic from the ethical standpoint and shows us the moral necessity of mysticism. His treatment of "Psychim and Supra-psychism" in the 8th chapter is profound.

I have referred to a part of the book chapter by chapter after the manner of a reviewer only to give the reader an idea of the variety and magnitude of the author's contributions to a vitally important problem. In composing the book Dr. Sircar has harnessed the whole of the relevant Western Philosophy represented by Hegel, Bergson and others in his service and has made fresh, stimulating and pregnant contributions of his own.

The Bharatiya Kala Prakashan has done very useful work by undertaking the publication of this valuable volume which is expected to be a distinct addition to world's stock of knowledge on the subject of mysticism from the Vaiṣṇavic and Tāntrik standpoints.

—N.N. SIRCAR

Preface

The publication of the present work represents a part of the comprehensive scheme. In brief, the whole scheme is as follows—(1) Establishment of Schools and Colleges of various types for imparting education in all branches of human knowledge, grouped together on all extensive plot of land by the side of the Ganges in a few miles from Calcutta. (2) Establishment of different allied bodies *viz.*, Vedic, Jaina, Buddha, Śikh Pariṣats etc. (3) Publication of model Text books on various subjects incorporated in its curriculum for the benefit of students (4) Publication of Extension Lectures delivered by specialists in different subjects. The activities under the first three heads needs not by dwelt on here as they are given in detail. Some reference to the activities under the fourth head may not be out of place.

The present book is dwelling with Vaiṣṇavism and Tāntricism. It consists of Eighteen Lectures on Vaiṣṇavism and the Ninteenth chapter is on Tāntricism by Dr. M.N. Sircar, a scholar of international reputation, many of whose monumental works on Philosophy and Religion are already in the field. These are delivered as "Śrī Kṛṣṇa" Extension Lectures on "Aryan Dharma," The author himself, a mystic, is fit to deal with the theme and he has done thorough justice to it by his masterly and exhaustive treatment in a lucid style, so that the subject though abstruse, has been made interesting and intelligible.

Such publications of our Religion may be compared both in its aim and spirit to similar publications of lectures on Comparative Religion delivered under different Trusts in the West as well as in the East; and we venture to believe that this book will be a distinct contribution to World Thought and Culture for a proper understanding of the grandeur, depth and dignity of Hindu Mysticism, or properly speaking Aryan Mysticism, as embodied in the Sacred Literature of the Aryans.

We are thankful to Sir N.N. Sircar, K.C.S.I., for contributing a Foreword and materially helping us in the publication.

It is hoped that the publication will meet with a ready and warm reception both in this land and abroad, both from the lay public interested in Religion and from the specialists who have made a technical study of the subject.

—S.C. Seal

INTRODUCTION

This volume is a sequel to my Hindu Mysticism (according to the Upāniṣads). It presents the dynamic forms of Mysticism, Vaiṣṇavism and Tāntricism. Professor Bergson in his two essays on Religion and Morality has wrongly characterised Hindu religion as purely statical. Hindu Mysticism has its emphasis upon transcendence where the movement of life is eased in the cosmic stirring of a spirit. Dynamic Mysticism fully bears it out and presents the wider, the freer movement of life and consciousness. Vaiṣṇavism forms by itself a distinct mode of thought and spirituality. It has a philosophic setting and spiritual inspiration distinct from the Tantras, though it is regarded as an Ācāra (spiritual discipline) in the Tantras.

The arrangement of the topics and the presentation are free, following the spirit and the inspiration rather than the details of techings; for Mysticism, more than anything else, is a live inspiration. A distinct sympathy is more important and helpful for its understanding than reference to the literatures that have grown about the systems. There is a vast literature on the subject, specially on the Tantras, but the fundamental structure of though and spirituality is almost the same. And I feel that unless the structure is followed closely with creative sympathy and spiritual imagination, it is difficult to follow the meaning and significance of the teachings. Mysticism deals with Life in its utmost stress of creative expression and Being in its unfathomable stillness. It emphasises the Mystery of Silence along with the Mystery of Life.

Mysticism creates intense interest as it represents the effort of the human spirit to move on its wings of scale the graded universes of existence. This interest does never vanish as it acquaints us with the symphonies of life that are hidden deep in it. The realised soul becomes a piece of living poetry, beauteous in form, rythmical in the beats of being. The Mystic enthroned in the majesty of the Infinite Being and ineffable Peace, his foot-prints are left on the canvas of space and time. He comprises are universe within himself fully realising the living contact of his wider being with every atom of existence. He has the unique experience of the irridiscence of light, the efflorescence of bliss, the ease of life and the cosmic stirring of will. This inestimable privilege is his by his sleepless effort at the conquest of the intractableness of matter and his endless struggle to shake off his finitude. He is led to this supreme puissance by an unconscious but irresistible drive.

Inspite of the realistic bent of though and the melioristic attitude of life, mysticism still has its hold today because it lifts the veil from inmost secrets of being and it offers experiences too deep for words, far beyond thought. Such expeiences are in the beginning occasional, but with the maturity of fitness they become continuous. Religion, to quote Collingwood, "is not a superfluity for the educated and an opiate for the masses." "It is the only known explosive in the economy of that delicate internal-combustion engine, the human mind. People rich in religious energy can overcome all obstacles and attain any height in the scale of civilization." Mysticism is still a close preserve to logical intellect, its organum is not as yet disclosed. It is not knowledge. It is super-knowledge. it is not knowing. It is being.

No one is better aware than the author of the difficulty of the task and his incompetence to deal with a subject so vast, and mysteries so deep, but a secret and persistent urge compels him to bring out the ancient Wisdom with the fervent hope that some few will appreciate the ancient treasure, even when the waves of the troubled sea of modern thought do not allow us to hold our anchor of life in Spirit.

—M.N. SIRCAR

CONTENTS

CHAPTER-I

Reason, Revelation and Faith

Religion is not reflection on life. It is the sympathetic understanding of life. It is living experience. It is direct contact with living Reality. It is its appraisement through every channel of experience, and therefore it emanates from the rhythm of our whole being. The full nature of religion is difficult to understand, for sympathetic understanding varies in proposition to our responsiveness to the rhythm of life. The variation in spiritual experience is relative to the degrees of receptively. Spiritual life is insight, reception and adaptibility. It is very difficult to fix its form as we become responsive in the different parts of our being with different degrees of intensity.

Religious experience is unique, for it proceeds directly from the wise passiveness of the soul; it is essentially identified with life, and the more life opens into its sublime immensities, the more does it yield its nature and reveal its reality. This living experience is not a matter for reason to judge or to appreciate, for in its finer vibrations and genial currents, thinking has no place. Understanding builds up a scheme of knowledge and can hardly envisage the spiritual heights of our being and the richness of our experience. Reflection on spiritual experience is not religion. Reflection leaves us cold and indifferent and cannot give the joyousness of spirit. It can only give us the intellectual chart of spiritual life, which affords, at best the foundation of faith in the light of reason. It has to forgo the living foundation of faith. Reason examines the condition and the possibility of faith and enters into fruitless discussion whether the life of faith is consistent with the life of knowledge. The controversy has its origin in the atempt at rationalising faith, quite, ignoring the fact that faith has a higher orientation than reason, as it is associated with life. Reason discovers that dynamic relativity is involved in its nature, and in this sees the basis of a spiritual life. But to say that spiritual life has in it a polarity of the finite and the infinite and to accept it as the rational basis of faith do not go far to indicate the nature of that life. And it is naturally so, for reason cannot rise above its own nature and enter into the heart of things. Reason can see the setting, but cannot enter into the innate experiences imbibed in the life of spirit. Understanding is the least part of religion. It is essentially experience, the sense of numen.

The conflict of faith and reason is the conflict between life and understanding. And this conflict is due to the enforced division between the two. Understanding apart from life can raise a schema of faith, but in this construction we forget that life has its inner movements which reason cannot penetrate. To characterise religion as the immergence into eternal life is the least understanding of it. The touch and the impress of the Divine upon the dedicated spirit cannot be appraised exactly by reason. It is a living experience.

Spiritual life is appealing because of its richness, because of its responsiveness to life, it is essentially life in its finest expression. Spiritual life develops its own understanding an understanding that sees the immediate presentation of experiences and their orchestral unity. And in it the joyousness, the security of faith goes with knowledge. Religious experience is the complete presentation of life and naturally religious life cannot be a life without a deep appeal to the foundation of our nature. And indeed it is a truism that in spiritual experiences our nature gets the fullest satisfaction, for here the faculties of the soul are presented in their best form and in finest intensity.

Religious experience presents life in all its integrity and completeness. It is a life rich in every way, rich in vividness of feelings and rich in magnitude and qualities. Hence reason, divinely tuned, instead of building up a schema finds in it a rhythm which can present the transcendental truths. Life in its finest urge does not leave any side of our nature unpresented; it exhibits the transcendental truths and at the same time indicates life's movements towards the assimilation of them in life's completeness. Religion has no meaning, if it is detached from Truth; the life of faith and the life of reason in their rhythm combine to present and enjoy the heighest Truth which is also the greatest Holiness. They present the two sides of the one integral experience; reason, the setting in its immediateness, faith, the core of spirit.

Religious life is the life of transcendental knowledge, beauty and holiness. It makes our life full and intense at every point, and the difference that is sometimes emphasised between these experiences emanates from the absence of integral faith and experience. When the fuller harmony of life is active, all the aspects of life become effective. Reason in its rhythm appraises Truth, faith in its rhythm finds the greatest security, love in its rhythm appreciate the finest joy, eternal life and movement. The spiritual life does not leave any side of our nature blank, for it is fuller life, finer delight, and greater truth.

If spiritual life is assuredly finer life and wider experience, naturally it will go with revelation, for revelation is emanation of truths from the deep recesses of being. The word 'revelation' these days has lost its grace, as it points to a supra-rational source of knowldge. And since revelation is associated with the life history of a particular personality, it naturally loses its force. It makes great demand upon faith and credulity. In the great historical religions, save and except Hinduism, 'Revelation' takes place through some historical person, and hence naturally, with all the respect shown to his life, character and utterance, human reason has tried to find out the rational basis of faith, for revelation requires the surrender of reason and the ready acceptance of a truth not otherwise accessible. And sometimes the revealed texts give so diametrically opposite opinions concerning the fundamentals of life that it becomes almost impossible to assess their values properly.

Such difficulties are natural when the source of knowledge becomes extra-ordinary and uncommon. These difficulties are greatly enhanced by emphasising the externality of revelation and its source. The human mind is accustomed to think of revelation as a source of knowledge quite external to our mental formations; and at times new truths visit us if it pleases God. The idea of a distant Divinity makes revelation more an accident—and a happy accident—than a possibility ingrained in our nature. This outwardness of revelation is what reason finds difficult to grasp, for it enforces a division between human experience, human reason and Divine wisdom. But this difficulty is immediately removed, if the inwardness of revelation and its inherent association with life is fully reaslised. If instead of the conception of a distant Divinity sending forth His message in auspicious moments of life, life is looked upon as conceived and sustained in Divinity, revelation will mean a new flash of light, a new flow in life. Revelation is really the presentation of a finer and greater Truth from the supra-sensuous and the supra-mental, but it does not mean that it is quite foreign to life; it is in it and it emanates from the finer urges of life. The finest truths are given out where the movement of life is delicate and the urge subtle. It is, to cull a phrase from the mystic Ruysbroeck, "radiance above reason."

Revelation implies the presentation of Truth not otherwise accessible. Life has its inward guidance, and when the inward guidance emanates from the super-mind, life receives the light of revelation. All the indications of life are not revelations. Indications may proceed from our vital and instinctive nature. Indications may come from the mind and higher intelligence. They are formations in the different layers of our beings. They do not proceed from the fountain source, from the encompassing super-mind. The impress of the super-mind upon life makes life radiant in joy, silent in peace, and luminous in knowledge. This super-mind contains supra-mental truths, which life constantly aspires to realise.

Intuitions have great values, since they are the fine indications immanent in life. They reveal the secrets that are accessible in the ordinary course of development. But revelations are truths that become accessible only when the supra-mental urge becomes active. Intuitions are possible to the sensitive, revelations, only to the elect. Revelation, therefore, implies a special fitness. Since this fitness is not everywhere present, revelation can be only possible in select cases.

Revelation is not psychic intuition. There are occasions where they psychic fitness exhibits some inner truths. The poetic, the artistic inspiration emanates from psychic transparence and responsiveness, but that necessarily is not revelation; even the fine philosophic constructions are deep laid in the psychic layers of our being; but they are not revelations.

Revelation must not be confounded with intuitions

proceeding from the different layers of our being. There are vital intuitions, expressing the truth and the law of vital being; there are mental intuitions, proceeding from the mental being, there are intuitions of the higher mind, revealing to us the ideas of reason, the archetypal forms, and sometimes the archetypal beauties. These intutitions are still within the range of our own experience and cannot really pass for revelation. Revelation supposes a direct touch with either the over-mind or the super-mind. It really presuppose the expression of spirit quite independent of vital or mental functioning. These are truths covered in the light of spirit, but which cannot be felt and realised unless life can forgo its natural limitations and formations and can invite its radiant and beatific nature.

Revelation has direct connexion with our psychic nature and psychic harmony, but its essential character lies in its objectivity and its objective impress. It is not a subjective intuition, or feeling. The self receives an impress from an inaccessible height. The psychic life in man is continuous with the cosmic life, and the psychic openings acquaint us with the radiations that emanate from the cosmic. And this accounts for illuminations more subtle than psychic intuitions. The psychic intuition may proceed from the urges of our vital and psychic being; these urges are indications of the prospective vital or mental growth; the psychic life cannot ordinarily rise to a fineness to understand and feel the thread of connexion between it and the cosmic life. Psychic intuition cannot in every case reveal the supra-mental truths and purpose in the movements of life. But in cases where the psychic penetration is deep enough to be responsive to the cosmic urges, it reaches the wider range of knowledge, realises the greater posibilities of life and feels the deeper cosmic movements. Revelations introduces to us an aspect of life which is not otherwise accessible. The psychic fitness acquaints us with the vital and creative forces, with the idea-forces, with generic volitions. It emanates from the layers of our psychic life; but when the supra-mental intuition reveals the cosmic life, we are then entitled to get a glimpse of the transcendent truths and the formations of the transcendental will. In revelation, therefore, the mind oversteps its own limitations and becomes free from the obscurities of its nature and with finer responsiveness it gets sure access to the Divine wisdom. Super-mental revelation, therefore, carries higher authority, for, it originates from a source that cannot deceive and impresses through an organ that cannot err. It is, as William James says, "cosmic pure experience."

Every man does not possess equal psychic fineness. Every soul does not receive in the same way, and naturally there arises divergence of opinion about revelations and all reveltions will not point to the same truth. Revelations proceed from the graded universes; there is a vast range of cosmic life hidden from us and unless the psychic perception can reach the highest pinnacle of supra-mental life, the finest revelations canot be obtained. The spiritual life appears, therefore, in the beginning as the growth of the finest possibilities, for the spiritual life is really an opening to the finer ranges of experience—but unless the phychic life can catch the main spring of the cosmic life, life cannot enjoy the true revelations of spirit. Insight into graded worlds and revelation are, therefore, to be distinguished. The former is true to its own sphere, the latter only to the Divine. The Divine wisdom, therefore, must proceed direct from the divine source and not from any finer layer of being; these flashes open to us ranges of existence, but they do not reveal the Divine life in its immanence or in its transcendence.

Life is exposed to error in almost all the stages of its expression and naturally in our upward ascent unless the mind can distinguish the expression and the divided urges from the main spring of the supra-mental current, it has every chance of mistaking the shadow for the reality. This emphasis at once distinguishes revelations from the other urges of life, however fine and radiant. The tendency of the age to explain spiritual life as a sublimation of sex impulse is an illustration of this usual fallacy

The vital urges, however refined, cannot pass for the urges of spirit. The spiritual urge touches all part of our being and transforms the instincts to its advantage and removes the division of nature and being. The fundamental deficiency in the modern interpretation of religion lies in its enforced divorce from its fountain source. To explain religion as the finer manifestation of the vital or the psychic urge is really to miss its true nature and import.

The spiritual urge is the finest urge. The vital and the mental urges are obstructed expression of spirit and consciousness. It is easier to conceive the finer gradations of life as more original than to conceive them as evolved by a pressing urge. This urge is rather the prop of a finer life, which is exhibited under resistance and pressure. But that does not mean that the fine is less original and newly evolved. The resistance felt by the finer urge for its expression is clear proof that creative expression is the moulding of the gross by the delicate impress of life. The ordinary dualistic consciousness conceives the moulding of life in this way, but the fine and the gross are equally the urges of life. The one is the more expressive and elastic and the other less expressive and less elastic. Life is elasticity and expression, and where these indications are finest,—life has the best exhibition and the richest experience. In the ascending scale of expression, the restricting and seemingly dualistic character is removed.

The conflict between science and religion has been due to the pre-conceived notions of science and the want of fine psychological experiences. Science in its experimental analysis may ultimately reach the radiation of energies, but the psychological revelations of the finer form of energies remain to it for ever sealed. Hence in its interpretation of religion, it naturally starts from below and attempts an interpretation of superior experiences in terms of lower categories. However, the scientist cannot successfully explain them. These emergences really indicate finer realities which are not revealed because of the restricting influence of the forces. The psychological revelations assert the truth, for they exhibit the gradations of forces in a hierarchy and their regulation from the centre. The conflict between science and religion will always remain and the interpretation of religion in terms of science will be natural so long as the finer psychological experiences do not help us. They can alone convince us that there are finer forms of energies which do not necessarily emerge or are not radiations from the cruder forms working in the lower levels of existence. The physical the vital, the psychical, the spiritual are all expressions of the Primal Energy and to explain the spiritual in terms of the physical or the vital is not a guide to better understanding.

The spiritual is indeed superior to the vital and the physical urges, but this superiority does not indicate its difference in kind. Difficulty arises from the categorical fixation and differentiation of the spiritual from the material and the vital. The emergence of spirit out of matter or energy makes science bad and religion worse; the concept of energy with which the theory begins is not clearly defined, and the emergence of the finer out of the crude is not satisfactorily explained.

The trace of the original duality of mind and matter is still retained in some form, and this has been the cause of the separation of religion from science. The Indian mind has not experienced this conflict, for it has conceived supra-material and supra-mental forms of energy.

The material is spiritual; only, it is the restriction of the spiritual will or force. Bergson conceives matter as an inversion of movement of the 'Elan Vital'. Similrly it can be said that matter is not really an entity, it is the restricted movement of the Primal Will. It is easier to start with the primal will and to explain the physical as the concentrated vibrations of the spiritual, as the primal energy deflicts from the centre, than to start with the crude conception of energy or matter and to evolve finer expressions and energies out of it. And it is inconsistent with spiritual expeiences of ages, for spirituality presents a finer life, radiant vibrations, and luminous expression of the Primal Energy which are not experienced in the vital-physical world. Even the clear and the confused mental perceptions are an indication, that the primal energy has its degrees of expression which are not equally fine everywhere. This can explain that in the order of creative expression, the primal energy passes into grosser forms as it passes through the process of condensation and concentration. And this can only integrate the spiritual experiences with other forms of experience and can trace out a continuity between the levels of our consciousness on the one hand and the grades of existence on the other.

Indian spirituality, therefore, conceives the diffusion and the concentration of energy. Concentration goes with creative expression, diffusion with spiritual expansion. When the creative energy is suspended, the primary energy enjoys a transcendent poise. The Indian teachers conceive the three-fold modification of energy,—causal, subtle and gross. They represent the degrees of condensation. In the process of condensation, life grows in variety and complexity, but its fineness and subtlety suffers. The emergence of fine subtleties is, no doubt, a pleasing experience. Spiritual experiences are welcomed by modern scientific men as exhibiting the finer modulations of energy. But the finer modifications are not new and quite unexpected expressions, they are immanent in the crude forms and do not make a fresh start.

Some scientists cannot see the subtler movements of energy and hence conceive an advance in evolution in the spiritual and the mental; it is not an advance in the sense of a new category coming into existence. It is an advance in the sense of exhibition of the finerand the causal.

Religion is not therefore anti-scientific, it is rather super-scientific. Human experience can not always rise above the limitation of sense-intelligence, it can not see the immanence of the spiritual dynamism in the expression of life. But these supra-sensuous expressions of a spiritual dynamism become quite manifest to the intuitive (or seeing) intelligence. Subtle movements of dynamism become then evident and the physical is then realised as really the limitation of the spiritual.

Spiritual experience, instead of denying science, rather gives correct insight into and finally idealises it. It increases interest by demonstrating the deep-laid connexion with the different sides of existence and the common thread of life running through them. Science, in confining itself to a specialised universe, has really gone not further then establishing connexion between events of a statical universe—it cannot see the deep stress or stir that is moving in the heart of reality. Bergson perceives the shortness of this mechanised conception, for it touches the fringe of life and satifies itself with reducing the facts to fixed order and inflexible determinism ignoring the free creative energy. The dominating influence of science invades philosophy, which systematises conclusions of science in an ordered universe. Philosophy then becomes fond of scientific methods and raises up its structure on a statical conception of relations quite ignoring that living reality cannot be truly apprehended by scientific analysis. The new scientific out-look has its hopeful inspiration. The Indian out-look is comprehensive and synthetic. It has all along laid much emphasis upon the method of viewing things in integrity; for to view an event in isolation is not the correct understanding of it. It has a history and a back-ground, its correct appraisement is possible when that history and the strees under which it evolves are presented.

Bergson's liberation of philosophy from the thraldom of intellect has not only created a new interest in philosophy; it has reinstated religion. He gives emancipation from the fog of 'relativity of knowledge' and introduces us into the continuity of creative life, into the reality of history and emergence. What is life but creative urge and faith? This eternity of life is what man is always after; it has been the promise of religion. It is not reserved alone for a spiritual aristocracy, but is also meant for a spiritual democracy. To understand life sympathetically is to live religion.

The appeal of religion is really the appeal of life. *Sub-specie durationis* is the source of a new inspiration. The eternal joy of a creative life takes the place of joy of seeling things in their unchangeable fixity. Life remains to Bergson the source of eternal inspiration, for life is what transcends the continuous formation and is the reality. The religious sense would affiliate itself to life; religion is especially the instinct to appreciate and enjoy life apart from its form. This promises immortality. Life's formation undergoes changes, but not the stress, the impact which lies in the heart of things. And this *sub-specic durationis* is a rare vision, becuase it gives the knowledge of unfettered becoming. No terminal experience is possible in the process. Life is unceasing movement. Any terminal experience stops its flow and kills it. Religious enthusiasm certainly lies in enjoying the freedom of life and essentially in our release from the overpowering inertia of matter.

No doubt, in spiritual life there is an incessant urge of breaking all inertia, so that life can express its finest and best. But in this ascent there is an objective, and religion cannot transcend this *objectivity*. A ceaseless life, with every insistence to transcend the formation, sounds poetic, but it cannot convey turly the significance of spiritual life. The great attraction of spiritual life is its freedom from the sense of time; religion more than anything else has this appeal to *timelessness*. An appeal, no doubt, is there for eternal life, but eternity of life alone is not the greatest spiritual appeal and attraction.

In the spiritual ascent, though the sense of eternal life is made clear in every forward step, still the final realisation follows that kind of unique experience where the soul transcends completely the formative force of time. Professor Muirhead (Hibbert Journal, October, 1934) says "I seem to see also that unless we are further prepared to take timelessness with equal seriousness, unless we have the faith that in these experiences, we are realising values which transcend all time relations, and which are, in more than a rhetorical sense, eternal and uncreated, we are depriving them of their fullest, perhaps of all their meaning." In spiritual life there is a constant urge of unfolding, and this is a great attraction and offers exquisite felicities, but the greatest attraction of spiritual life comes from the promise of release from the time-sense and evolution. Evolution in spiritual life is not the final promise, though life passes through successive stages of growth to a stage where the whole existence is experienced instantaneously, without any reference to time-sense. Spiritual intuition, as distinguished from mental, must reflect existence in its supra-mental, mental, vital and physical expression, life in its immanence and transcendence simultaneously, for spiritual insight is the insight into the whole, and this insight makes us free from the restricting sense of time.

The expansive vision of spirit is really the effort to go beyond time and to enjoy life in its timelessness. The vital intuitions are in time, the process of the emergence and the expression of life are in time. Bergson has done his best to emphasise the eternal urge of life, still he has not been able to transcend the continuity of Time in the timeless Eternity revealed in the moment of mystical exaltation. The emergence of life in its supreme beauties and sublime dignities makes, no doubt, an appeal to romantic feelings. A deeper urge is indicated in the attempt to realise the permanent and the eternal values, which cannot be influenced by time. The spiritual life is more attracted to the ever-present, than to the ever-creative.

The Divine life may reveal finer, still freer movement, for it means the upward ascent from earthly sense to heavenly wisdom. In its purest essence it must not only be satisfied with the irrepressible creative urge, but must find out the deep harmony of the soul, where the creative urge gives place to the illumined silence. Bergson has been so much influenced by the formative vital force that he cannot visualise the finer intuitions which give the synoptic view of reality and reveal the superior strata of being beyond the operations of Time and beyound Time itself. Time is associated with spiritual life, so long as spiritual force is looked upon as a moulding power; but to identify spirit completely with Elan

Vital or Duration is to over-look the nature of spirit which is enduring and beyond the influence of Time. In its widest commonalty of transparent and luminous being, time plays no part; for there is no creative urge, though there is intensive expression. Our mind, as it is constituted, cannot think without the help of time, and hence it is difficult for it to understand the range of life not covered by time. Bergson has characterised intellect as spatialised; if intellect is spatialised, mind is temporalised. The mental movement is in time, and mind can hardly conceive transcendence of time.

Memory is the fundamental characteristic of mental life. It reveals the history of mental life. Memory can understand movement, for it is essentially *associated* with movement and integrates the past with the future. Mental intuitions are in time. The intuitions of mind are of various kinds. The vital-mind presents intuitions in time essentially and presents the functioning of the vital-mind forces through time; but the vital-mind cannot understand the more delicate impress from the super-mind and cannot truly interpret revelation which presupposes the existence of the super-mind.

Life has its subtle revelations but these are indications of the higher and finer phases of consciousness than of *Elan-Vital*. Bergson, by ignoring the eternal consciousness associated with life, has shut the door upon revelation. The finer premonitions and indications in life's growth may be embraced by our vital life. The vital movements are not entirely vital and blind. Consciousness is immanent in every movement of life, though the clear emergence of it can be traced in the supra-vital expression. In vital life revelation can have no meaning; there is indeed the clear indication of future development in vital life—it is a possibility which it enjoys with evolution—but this indication of future development and progress is an indication of life, but is not revelation.

Revelation implies the positive working of the higher mind in its fine luminosity, for it can take place where life becomes free from the depressing influence of crude matter. It, therefore, comes at a stage late in the evolutionary ascent, but it does not mean any external influence, or any outward impress; it certainly implies the impress from the subtle upon the less subtle, for it is really the occasional visitation from the higher and the finer which is deep-laid in life. When therefore, life expresses itself in its higher phases, light streams forth to help the upward ascent.

Evolution does not mean the life moves on without leaving a record behind. The urge and the indication imply that in life there is an inward necesity and a law to guide its ascent or descent, for nothing in life is capricious or accidental; evolution is really a movement to assimilate or better to express the higher and the finer movements of life, and this higher is laid in it and is not the one coming into existence by the pressure of onward movement.

Life in its creative evolution is passing through a process of concentration, but a wide expanse is always behind it, and is always immanent in it. Revelation is the occasional infusion of a broader vision and a greater spirit for the better moulding of life. Revelation is like the stream of light which enlightens the otherwise dark canvass of life.

The synthesis which reason sets up is, therefore, symbolic and pictorial. The religious instinct cannot be satisfied with it; hence the aspiration in us is to go beyond this scaffolding of reason to the world of faith; religion, far above anything, demanding the presentation of life in its finer formations. It can not be satisfied with an ideology behind it. And in this widening of experience, revelation plays a great part.

The supra-mental truths are indeed truths immanent in spirit. They can never be exposed, until life grows aspirant after them. In the movement of life, finer truths are revealed with chastened being; and the supra-mental dynamism can therefore be conceived as the purest from of life. As life descends in scale its fineness is obscured by inertia and ignorance. And, therefore, religious life implies a direct inspiration and reception from the living God, beyond the functioning of the vital or the mental, or the higher mental. Since the finest psychic life is not generally operative in us, we are given to interpret revelation as something external, when there are occasional glimpses from the heights of life.

Our psychic life touches the vital, the vital-mental, the mental-spiritual, the spiritual; and because the higher ranges of the psychic life are not still within the scope of ordinary perception, they are given upto doubt and scepticism. And whatever is received in the twilight of the super-conscious is accepted as accidental happy visitation from the remote cornor of conscious life. The conscious life has a wide circumstance, all parts of which still remain unillumined, and many amazing incidents in great lives are only intrusions of light from the deeper layers of being.

Evolution of life indicates the secret urges, well-laid in our nature, and if the thread of life could be traced in its finer aspects, it will be seen to be associated with *revelation* almost at every step. A happy opening of the psychic life indicates its presence there. And because there is an inconscient nature in man it cannot allow the impress of higher truths and hence revelation appears as influencing life from a distance. Truth is otherwise. A new vista, which is sure to throw much light on the problem, has been opened in the new psychology of the unconscious. The world 'unconscious' has a wide range of meaning and it is not as yet definite what it does and does not include in its scope. It has been accepted as supplying the lost key to the explanation of all kinds of experiences, from the abnormal to the super-normal. The psychology of the super-conscious is still to be studied seriously before the mysteries of the spirit can be *apprehended.* Psycho-analysis has sought to explain the conscious in the light of the *'unconscious'*, which, to it, is more living, more potential and more comprehensive, as it contains the chief spring of our mental life.

The 'unconscious' is not necessarily the life of instinctive urges; it includes within it the super-conscious forces. There is the finer and more expansive, the grosser and the more restricted movement in the psyche. The spiritual is distinct from the vital in its fine luminosity and great comprehensive-ness. The whole gamut of the psychic life is divided into different ranges and expressions, but the higher scale gives better harmonies and more delightful super-conscient depths of being.

The unconsious, therefore, not only implies the subconscious deeps of being, but also the super-conscient reaches. The whole mystery of life is locked up in the psyche, and the grades of life have apparent differences because of the brightness or the dimness of psychic expression. The instinctive urges, seen by themselves, are simply vital, but read in continuity with the supra-mental, have a spiritual significance as they have a purpose in the economy of life. The supramental has a direct connexion with the vital, which, at times becomes instrucmental to the expression of the supra-mental in the vital plane and order. Revelation is an opening in the unconscious in its supra-mental ranges. The supra-mental indications are called revelations, because they are unfamiliar and reveal truths beyond the mental gaze and reflection, they proceed from the psychic depths. And, they are, therefore, differentiated from the finer mental and vital intuitions; for the movement of the psyche in its finest form is not within the easy access of humanity in the present scale of evolution.

Evolution is being regulated, moulded and directed by the invisible force, the unconscious promptings of the soul, and when the higher organs of reception become active, they feel the touch and the revelations of the supra-mental shaping power and wisdom.

The natural lines of evolution are indicated in the urges of life; the urges to supra-mental evolution and super-normal expressions are also immanent in life, but their existance and functioning are not evident, becuase life is not as yet active in these stages. Hence, a sudden flash from the great heights of conscious life looks like a miraculous event streaming forth from an external source. But really revelations manifest the finer truths of the subtler evolution of life. And at every step of its development, the inward light reflects its guidance; and this light proceeds from the transparent psyche, which has almost infinite range and various shades of luminous expression. Plato could trace the sufficiency of the ideas to Psyche. "They (the ideas) obtain life and motion by their entertainment in a living intelligence. Such a living intelligence with its gaze fixed upon ideas was what Plato termed a psyche. He conceives of a basic Psyche whole active grasp of ideas conditions impartially the whole proess of the universe. This is the Supreme Craftsman, on whom depends that degree of orderliness which the world exhibits. There is a perfection in this Psyche, which Plato finds, beyond his power to explain." Plato also speaks of Eros, 'the soul in the enjoyment of its creative function....., 'the urge towards ideal perfection.[1]

The whole cosmic evolution including the evolution of man is a process that is controlled and directed by this invisible principle, Psyche, and Plato traces out the cosmic character of the Psyche. The psyche of man is in intimate association with the cosmic psyche and the evolution of spiritual life implies the energising of the psyche, its release from the vital and the mental movements of life. This free movement of the psyche realises its intimate relation with Cosmic Psyche and can participate with its cosmic movements. This indeed is the final promise in spiritual life; but the awakening and the free activity of the psyche is the real beginning of it. Mysterious indeed is the plain in spiritual life. The gentle awakening of and correct aspiration in psychic life immediately make it possible for the individual to appraise the reality and the promise of the cosmic oscillations of the universal psyche.

Revelation is really the impress of these cosmic oscillations, in as much as it bears upon us the truth, the force of the power which is at the root of life. In the psychic depth, one can feel the underlying connexion and the living touch of this power, and when its working can be appraised consciously and its interference is welcomed reverently, we can then understand the meaning and the helpfulness of revelation. Revelation throws saving light on the soul; and at a stage of new development life requires the new light which emerges from the cosmic depths. Streams of light, not otherwise accessible, flow from these heights. They sometimes appear strange, because we are not acquiainted with the full possibilities of the psychic life. The psyche,

1. Whitehead's Adventure of Ideas—Science and Philosophy.

as yet, has not been discovered by humanity in its full potentiality. Revelations, consequently, are challenged as affirma-tions of dogmatic theology. They are denied completely as they break the settled convictions based upon reason and introduce the miraculous element in religion. In truth, revelation instead of undermining the settled convictions of reason regarding the Divine, really restores the living God to man; for reason in its earnest attempt to put up a natural theology can hardly satisfy the finest spiritual aspiration,—the touch and the communion with the living soul; and revelation, instead of introducing a miraculous element in religion, indicates the naturalness of spiritual life. It shows that life is broad-based upon the Divine; the divine element of knowledge is not an exception, but can be a rule, if the soul feels true dynamic aspiration.

Life is a free movement in spirit, and the laws which control the surface, hardly go to the spring. Miracle owes its origin to the ignorance of the creative spirit which infuses life with light at every stage of development. Life has its secret layers of expression and the laws working in them are indeed different from the laws working in the order of phenomena. Miracles are revelations of the finer forces. Their working is not always grasped by the mind, though they are not without causes. They are indications of the still higher stretches of life.

Any influence from them will appear a miracle to the untutored soul, for it is not quite aware of the movement of life or spirit or energy. The sudden introduction into the different planes of existence cannot help us to assimilate their plan and nature, and hence they are regarded as mysterious. The functioning of life in the universe has not been the same; the finer world of the super-mind, so long as we are not acquainted with the finer working of psyche, will appear as a mircle, for it will mean an occasional interference with the ordinary laws of evolution. But the finer vision will reveal a continuity between mental and super-mental psychism, and will trace out the truths of finer life due to the ingress of the super-mental dynamism. In truth, the evolution of life is regulated by the control of the finer, secret urges of a deeper life, and Plato is correct when he says that the psychic gives life to ideas, for the psyche is the fountain-spring of life.

This psyche is a continuous existence; wherever there is life, there is psyche. But its intensity is not the same every where; it cannot have uniformity in expression. It has different scales of luminosity, range, delicacy and sensitiveness. But its continuity can be everywhere traced. Our evolution is an ascent in the higher scale of psychic perfection, for the greater luminosity, elasticity and suppleness of the psyche give more delicate moulding, higher expression and greater wisdom.

The psyche in man is capable of infinite development, and the line of development can be well-indicated by the psychic tendencies. Matter, Life and Mind are connected with it; somewhere its expression is more suppressed, somewhere it is better expressed. In mind it has a fuller expression than in life, in life, fuller than in matter; in super-mind it has its luminous cosmic expression. When the psyche in man becomes consciously active, it receives new ranges of light and new movements of life. These are really revelations, which open to man new vistas of knowledge, new movements of life; under the pressure of these forces life rises into its finest forms, knowledge moves in the subtle world of ideas; and what was once a mere theory becomes a veritable fact with the growth of the fine psychism. In some cases, the guidance of life, and not only knowledge, is indicated in its refined movements. The psyche, when it is perfectly luminous, reveals the vastness of existence with its infinite varieties of expression. And realy the finest spiritual development implies the clear presentation of all the grades of existence moving in the rhythm of life and in the ether of delight.

Religion in its living and active sense, has a finer meaning and promise than science and philosophy. Science presents continuities and integrities that are true of a class of phenomena; it cannot dive deep into the mysteries of life which are not easy of access. Philosophy rises to the understanding of the integral existence, but it can not touch the thread of life that runs through all, for it has not the insight that is required to go direct into the mysteries of life.

No doubt, in the rhythmic movements of reason philosophy gives us the finer touches of life, but then it merges itself into religion. And hence a distinction is always drawn between reason and revelation, reason being understood in the ordinary dialectical sense. But when reason can get hold of the finer harmonies, hardly any difference is left between the two. Philosophy passes from thought into contemplation.

Science today is passing gradually into a mysterious universe by leaving off the rigid determinism of the surface-life and discovering the spontaneity of life. Both science and philosophy can only touch the fringe of the deeper existence, as the instruments they use are not calculated to lead them deep into the *mysteriorum mysterium*, for they are more positive in attitude and outlook, which can hardly help to divine the mysteries of life completely. It requires intellectual sympathy more than anything else to manifest the deeper secrets of life.

Revelation is necessarily welcome as presenting a finer

method for a better opening, for it is really a radiation in a moment of life's superior harmony. Religion goes with revelation, for its inspiration is really to make life unfold itself in its brighter from and higher grace. Religion has no serious meaning, if this appeal is lost. It not only gives wider knowledge, but helps fuller unfolding with the help of this knowledge. It exhibits life at its best, and hence the revelation of higher truths, brighter harmonies, fuller delights is associated with it. The promise of religion is eternal life, and revelation makes this promise good, for there is nothing besides it which can adduce better arguments for immortal life. Revelation transcends experience and reason, and manifests the direct hold of life. It has unique importance as a force of inspiration. Revelation is associated with the finest expression of life, it means the breaking of bondage of matter and sense, in which life is generally confined. Spirit in man cannot function effectively because of the touch of matter; the obscurities of the physical and the vital life do not allow the free expression of spirit.

The urges of the spirit are calm, expressive, wide and blissful; the urges of the vital are impetuous concentrated and impulsive. The vital is the great force on the physical plane; in the course of evolution of our spiritual life, the vital is gradually assimilated and transmuted in the spiritual. It does not lose its force, it loses its normal functioning and becomes the instrument of spiritual expression on the physical plane. The obscurities of the vital are removed and the vital currents work more joyously under the influence of spirit. When the vital is thus harmonised with the spiritual, revelation becomes natural and a constant phenomenon, for the obscurities are totally removed, allowing spirit its fullest expression and greater activity.

Revelation, indeed is the primary functioning of spirit.

And it is supposed supra-natural, because spirit is not consciously functioing in normal life, and hence when the descent of spirit takes place in us, it appears something quite new, and quite different from the normal functioning of the psychic dynamism.

In the usual functioning of psychic life, the finest part of it is not active generally and hence the finer dynamism of spirit looks like an intervention with the natural psychological laws. The truth, on the contrary, is, that with it our psychic life attains a higher pitch of activity manifesting the deeper secrets of life, which cannot be otherwise apprehended.

Revelation goes with the higher opening of life; hence it is in a sense, the finer knowledge of a finer world. And since of this world direct knowledge is not ordinarily possible, it has a value as a new source of knowledge, which does not deny but completes the knowledge commonly vouchsafed to man. And when it becomes natural and not occassional, it indicates the direct connexion with the comic consciousness implementing the otherwise defective knowledge through the senses.

Revelation puts a grace upon our life, for it exhibits life in its relation to the supra-mental and in the supra-mental light the values of life are changed. The contraries of normal life are transcended not by denying them, but by throwing a light upon them which can show their spiritual usefulness in the setting of life. But the greatest promise is that it can shed genial light upon the darkness of the soul, and endow us with light before which all the movements of life change their ordinary meaning and appear holy and beautiful. Its greatest service lies in exhibiting life in diviine reference and divine guidance.

When the psychic life is fully organised and finely developed then the stretches of the divine life open before us in all phases of its movement. But the highest knowledge is reached in a moment of revelation where the psyche no longer bears any difference with the Divine, but proceeds from fellowship to identity. It is a luminous and the finest experience in the psyche. Intellectual intuition, to be developed correctly, must necessarily presuppose psychic purity, transparence and not only philosophic reflection, for after all philosophic reflection can remove mental obscurities, but that is not enough for direct realisation.

The mental intuition that develops after critical reflection is not really spiritual intuition. The mental intuition is lower in rank and potentiality then the divine revelation; the one proceeds from our mental being, the other from the divine. Anything, coming directly from the Divine, has a distinct character. And the kind of intuition that is consequent upon philosophic reflection has a lower value than revelation; for it is an opening in the higher mind. Revelation goes deeper. It gives the highest *gnosis*. The mystic does not think, but sees; wonderfully enough a wide horizon of spiritual perspective opens to him and he is surrounded by exquisite and delightful experiences rising from every part of being; and he must have the unerring instinct enabling him to safely steer his course through the procession of inviting and absorbing psychic experiences till he reaches the end of pursuit, the terminus of being, where the focus of our consciousness becomes identified with the focus of universal consciousness. In mystical life their identification is the objective, though there is difference in the degree of identification. An acquaintance with the fringe of the Absolute consciousness is not enough, a direct and intimate identification can remove the limitation of knowledge and power and infuse the sense of a super-personality. In the ascending process the identification becomes increasingly established and each step forward is followed by a supersensuos realisation. We live in a progressively unfolding consciousness. But the finest experience is reached, when the centre of our consciousness is transferred to the Absolute, where our limiting or expansive experince vanishes completely in wideness and peace.

Hindu Mysticism acquaints us with reality. Actually it is a serious attempt to develop and organise our psychic being in order that the direct pathway to reality may be opened. This requires a new creative faith, a faith that sees more quickly and penetrates the fine working of our conscious life. It is the story of consciousness in its adventure of freedom and faith. In this sense it is approach to Truth and Reality.

CHAPTER-II

Contemplation and Rapport

There are two imperative demands in us, to know and to enjoy. The former is the demand of thought, the latter is the demand of life. Thought raises a construction out of the facts presented to experience not by empirical association, but by an architectonic process immanent in it. Philosophy presents this power of thought in its organic construction. It gives in its highest peneration the synthetic vision of reality. This synthetic vision endows reality with a certain liveliness and force, for synthesis is more than the bare presentation of details in integration. It makes out the *unique* character of reality, especially the living unity which it is and the living joy which it breathes. Whenever thought rises to this height, it abandons its barren skeleton and becomes something that is living and real.

Still thought does not exhibit the fully living character of reality, for the synthetic character which thought presents is more understood than felt and therefore it lacks the emotional content which religion implies and on which it thrives. The intellectual love of God is more than thought, it is amour wherein the spiritual consciousness emerges and acquaints us with Essence and Being. It is here that philosophic contemplation gives way to spiritual enthusiasm. A feeling of rapture gets hold of us, investing us with divine joy and grace. It introduces us to subtler movements of life, the aroma of peace, and spiritual blessedness. It would be the height of folly to suppose that mystical ecstacy is not the voice of a substantial harmony with the substance of things and with its movements. Professor Santayana says :—"Though substance may be forgotten, and only light and music may seem to remain, its massive harmonies in substance justify those mystical feelings, if anything justifies them at all. If all the spheres did not revolve according to law the morning stars would not sing together and the God of Aristotle would not think his eternal thoughts. Even enthusiasm, therefore, when not rarefied, expresses respect for substance and happy union with its motion." This indeed is a truism. This respect for substance and identification with its motion are what endow mystical life with its uniqueness and individuality. It is therefore not mere feeling nor an enthusiasm outflowing into rapid movements. Its proper development is associated with wide harmony, with ease of movement and wealth of being. The harmony of being with intensive adaptation is only natural to it. The adaptation becomes more complex, though at times it is not so much in evidence, because of the recoil of being upon itself in the height of realisation. This recoil is a necessity to make the wideness a living realisation and adaptation mobile.

The overflowing exuberance follows from the incompatiability of nature and spirit and the incapacity of nature to follow the indication and intimation of spirit. The finest exhibition of mystical life is possible when the least resistance put up by nature is removed and spirit gets easy and spontaneous expression; when the informating of spirit exceeds the capacity of reception through our psychic, mental, vital and physical being, the psycho-pathological phenomenon exhibits itself.

Though this adaptation and mobility are evident in mystical life, yet it must not be thought that mysticism does not afford occasional escape from the limitations and cares of life into ecstatic happiness. Santayana led by realistic instinct doubts the value of this kind of exaltation which to him is like standing apart from the current of life and the rejection of healthy and helpful realism.

True, mysticism acquaints us with the height of existence where the diastolic and systolic nature of life are suspended and which cannot be covered up by the insistences of life. Vital insistences may occupy a great portion of our being. But it would be the height of indiscretion to close the venues of diviner delights and refined wisdom by confining ourselves to active adaptations. The reach is removed from ordinary access, but that does not make it unworthy of pursuit. It is attractive, on the other hand, in as much as it affords relief from the tension of life. Even when activity follows contemplation, our being is forced to a great height and is led by spiritual impluse and not by animal instinct. A new source of energy is released which gives a new shape to our active expression and makes it spontaneous. Not only this, sometimes the feeling is definite that divine impulse becomes active which at once changes the meaning of our formations and adds a cosmic meaning to them.

This does not signify that Mysticism is a form of ideal construction and expression of creative intellect and creative will. The ideal construction follows the creative demand of our mental life and the ideal world is a mental formation but does not touch the still deeper currents of the spirit. Philosophy cannot rise above the mental construction. The ideal construction of Truth, Beauty and Holiness, however noble and lofty is the finest expression and our mind can make, but it touches only the fringe of the spirit. The stir of spirit can hardly be satisfied with the creative ideas of our mental life and the contemplation of values. It goes far beyond these values and their integration into a realm of supra-mental formation, into the transcendent depth of our being. There is the universe of the supra-mentallight and life formations, beyond our mental foramtion, and mysticism acquaints us with it. It cannot be equated by its nature with any kind of mental formation, however fine. It opens up new path-ways to spirit and its creative expression.

Mysticism makes its appearance when the sense of the *Numen* possesses us, over-comes us and introduces us into the mysteries of spirit. This sense of the Numen gives unique knowledge, since it throws a lurid light upon the inaccessible parts of our being.

This sense of the Numen makes out the difference between contemplation and rapport. Contemplation is the best mental effort revealing the truths and the values of the mental order. It affords the highest intellectual delight and intellectual effort. Its highest scale is reached when Existence is associated with Value, where the demands of our being are met by unfettered freedom. The bent of philosophic Mysticism has been towards the contemplation of the transcendent values, and the feeling it produces is one of meditative joy. Indeed philosophic mysticism has its bent towards intellectual intuition of the harmonious setting of existence and values. The sense of the Numen carries us beyond this philsophic contemplation of existence and values and invests us with the dynamic currents of the over-powering spirit and fiils us with divine life and holiness. The touch of spirit enlivens our being and introduces rapport, a divine rapture and exhiliaration. The holy spirit possesses us and takes hold of us and regulates all movements in us. This is the blessed *co-mingling* of life and spirit and is naturally believed to be more than the contemplation of existence and values. It is a kind of engrafting of a superior force which allows us to see more than what philosophic sense can endow us with, for it regulates our being with an ingress from inaccessible heights of the spirit.

This type of mysticism is dynamic. The emphasis upon the engrafting of spiritual force and investment of life with it opens a new chapter of realisation and experience and affords the understanding of the divine movements in life. Dynamic mysticism refuses to draw a distinction between the transcendent calmness and the movement of life. It sees life in illuminative silence as well as in its creative play and finds divine beauty and meaning in expression and enjoy the thrill it produces.

Dynamic mysticism takes hold of our entire being and its forces and endows them with a new meaning, force and power. They are exhibited in a new light that is not originally there. The light draws out their divine meaning, setting and radiance which they can not indicate but for a finer revelation in a higher plane of consciousness. No doubt, these have their dynamic significance, but they acquire a new light in being associated with the life and revelation of spirit. In this association we pass on from contemplation to rapture. The philosophic contemplation of Truth, Beauty and Goddness has its profundity, but the search of spirit gives an additional dignity and produces a rapport of the soul. This is not possible unless life rises to the height of appraising the forces in divine light. The intellectual contemplation produces a quiet, absorbing feeling. The Aesthetic contemplation invests the whole creation with a charm and an attraction infusing serene delight. The moral beatitude revels the order of creative ideals and values with its conquest of tension and resistance and its fine formation in the realm of ends.

But none of them affords the rapture of the soul, the divine rapport where spirit has engrosing impress which is more exquisite in delight than the contemplation of the values.

Nay, even the infusion of spirit adds a new dignity to the contemplation of ideals. And it becomes spontaneous. In the movement of spirit, the finest side of our nature comes to the fore, and our whole existence is exhibited with its hidden lustre. Beauty becomes more beautified, holiness becomes holier, truth acquires a divine meaning. Truth is not only the summit of existence, it is also the essence of spirit; beauty is the impress of spirit upon matter; power is the pressure of spirit upon vitality; light is the reflection of spirit upon mind. This touch of spirit does not obtain in the comtempiation of values, and does not make them so much absorbing and attractive. Spirit searches a new chord in our being and gives a new tune to it. To enjoy spirit in its creative expression and transfiguring power is what arrests our attention here. It is in short a transmutation of values. It cannot remain satisfied with the ideal movements. These satisfy the initial demands of our nature, but they cannot afford the felicity of the divine unfolding of life. In the ideal unfolding of life the sense, the mind, the intellect, and the will get their fine formation, but the inner man, in his substance and spirit, does not get his complete spiritual fulfilment. And therefore, the demand is still there for a divine unfolding, besides ideal unfolding; and with this demand the occasion arises for the spirituali-sation of our being in which man emerges as essentially divine in nature and existence which is temporarily shadowed. There is an inertia in our nature and the play of forces does not allow complete revelation of our nature as dynamically one with God.

The new life takes varieties of expression, and they depend upon the intensiveness of dynamic identification. The identification must be established in the central being because it gives the possibility of cosmic movements and provides for cosmic feeling. The ideal life also implies a re-orientation of our being, for the springs of action are not left to themselves; they come under the dictation and influence of the ideal self. The natural and the actual get a new formation by the force of the creative values. But this ideal formation is still mental. The formative force is the sense of worth or appreciation mentally conceived. The transvaluation of values is a higher order of expression of our moral and spiritual ardout and becomes possible when the transforming force proceeds directly from spirit. The cosmic power helps us to transcend the world of mental formation and valuation and introduces us to the realm of spiritual formation and valuation. This urge is cosmic in relation to the creative order. It is supra-cosmic when it exceeds creation. This becomes possible when the sense of the Numen and the transcendent Holy infuses its power within us and makes a direct revelation of the order of spirits. The normal moral or spiritual sense is here superseded by a super-normal spiritual sense, and personality gains a new consciousness, feels a new power and moves in the wake of the divine purpose. In this height of existence spirit exhibits absorption in rapport followed by intensive movement, when the energy, that is conserved, finds its release.

Rapport introduces the implication not only of a followship with spirit, but absorption into it. It is not the calm detached enjoyment of philosophic contemplation. It is rather pasing into divine passion and ecstacy wherein the joyous movement of the spirit is exhibited. It emits spiritual moods of various kinds. Ths is new revelation in the life of spirit, where the soul enjoys a unique feeling which is inexpressible in words. This rapport does not proceed from any definite part of our being, it is the expression of the whole being in identification with the beloved. In dynamic identification the divine spirit possesses the seeking soul and infuses it with its power and force. The aspirant soul passes into a unity in the active side of its nature, and enjoys the infinite modulations of spiritual harmony. Surely such a possession is not thought of an contemplation of even active ideals. The contemplation of values is a matter of transcendent reflection, but rapport is the actual identification with the divine spirit with all its creative expression.

In our investigation of truth, naturally a time comes when the growing self-consciousness in man steps beyond the realistic way of reception and the devious ways of thought, and encounters a supra-rational way by increasing its finer receptiveness and enlarging the range of his consciousness. And in this venture the mystic cannot be easily deceived, for the guidance he follows is the guidance of the unerring spirit.

The philosopher and the mystic start from the identical point, self-consciousnes, but while the philosopher limits himself to its normal functioning and intuitions, the mystic acquaints himself with its growing ranges and its subtler expansion and therefore his venture is the natural fulfilment of the enquiry into self-consciousness and its functioning. The philosopher encounters the natural opposition between the self and the not-self and cannot over-ride it, and therefore only views the sections of conscious life, leaving its wide range untouched. The mystic is more appealing, because he is more adventurous in withdrawing his consciousness from its natural limitations, and hence his claim is higher. The philosopher accepts the grades of knowledge as swnsuous, conceptual and intuitive. His task is a construction upon the former two; even when the demonstrates the contradictions involved in the nature of thought, he either takes his inspiration from the creative aspect of consciousness or takes his rest in the Absolute, thinking that contradictions are somewhere harmonised therein. But the philosopher is not sufficiently equipped to pass beyond the mental construction into the elastic life of spirit and to enjoy its delicate movements and subtle formations.

It is indeed a great privilege to be acquainted with the subtle turns in conscious life. The wider reaches of consciousness may understand better the laws of limited expression, its meaning, movements and force, and may finally educate and transform it by shedding its own light upon them. The continuity of life and its expression can then be seen in their finer gradation through the sub-conscious, the conscious and the super-conscious and the same thread of life can be traced through them; for they really present the same in its increasing elasticity and fineness. The law of foramtions in the lower movement of life then stands clear. Mysticism seizes upon the fine thread of consciousness to unlock the mysteries of existence. And in this attempt it has a scientific interest; for it unmasks the hidden depths of the supra-conscious life. Psychology cannot confine itself solely to normal mental activities, for whatever is conscious, is a matter of interest for psychology. The method that is followed is simple, for it is none other than introspection carried into the finer and higher reaches. The mystic is the self-experimenter, for his method is to give up conscious study and let the consciousness tell its own story in its wise passiveness. Really at this height aconsciousness is made free. Mysticism has its chief attraction in acquainting us with the cosmic ways and ends and in releasing us from the short ways of life. This is especially true of Indian Mysticism. Even in dynamic mysticism, this ideal has not been lost sight of. Though personality has been the chief basis or hold of mystical consciousness, the ideal is to get access ino the unfettered conscious life. The cosmic depths of existence with the free play of life has been the rock upon which mysticism fastens its anchor, the aspiration being the intimate acquaintance with the movement of life in infinite layers of existence. It is naturally this sympathy with the symphonies of life enjoyed in thieir concreteness as well as in their vastness that makes the mystical life a blessing and an attraction. Mystical life exhibits the unity of existence in a superior way; the details of existence are shown in the cosmic setting, and it is this knowledge and its ways that human mind in its profound aspiration must discover as the demand of our being. The real value of non-attachment lies in affording a release from the insurgent ways of life and in intimating us with the divine ways. Non-attachment releases us from the dubious ways and opens out the vistas of wider stretches of life. It affords release from the intellectual expression in art, history and philosophy and discloses new pathways of expression born of extreme detachment. Mysticism in all its forms, does not silence life and its creative expression; in some form, it emerges with a diviner synthetic note which pervades life. The mystical experiences are cosmical, these experiences are not cut off from our personal life. The personal here appears as the cosmical; at least, the dimension of our being and feelings show their cosmical nature for they are elevated to a super-mental plane where the character of our experience changes. The limitation of our experiences is withdrawn and our consciousness is released from its historicity and environmental setting. The opening of our consciousness on the higher levels does not mystify our experience, but show its wideness and infinite modulations. It is indeed the privilege of dynamic mysticism to respond to the vertical and the horizontal expressions of spirit and to accept and not to deny the details of existence and to read them with cosmic meaning and significance. The conflict and discord are dissolved as soon as the access into the fountain spring is attained. This is not a conceptual reading but a direct seeing into the heart of things.

Dynamic mysticism here in India has taken its chief expression in Vaiṣṇavism and in Tāntricism. Both of them have a philosophic approach to Truth, and inspite of the difference in the cast of thought, their unanimity lies in the emphasis put upon the dynamic aspect of existence and upon psychic harmony of being as yielding final insight and access. A fine poise of being with complete detachment from the usual ways may be a pre-requisite necessity. It does not follow a philosophic understanding or contemplation but the psychic tremor of the being. Dynamic mysticism relies more upon it than upon anything, for it reveals the mysteries of divine life which it is not possible for intellect to see and understand. Many things appear in dynamic mysticism (as indicated in Vaiṣṇavism and Tantricism) not sufficiently clear, because the psychic attitude necessary to appreciate them is not followed sincerely and not developed sufficiently. The intellectual background may be necessary to equip the understanding, but the psychic insight is required to enter into the mysteries of spirit and its expression and to enjoy them. A psychic unfolding may give us more than even we can imagine, and without this the depths of dynamic mysticism can hardly be followed and appreciated.

Dynamic mysticism may taken different forms, in as much as the identification is established with Elan Vital, or Will or Bliss. In Indian terminology the basic principle is either Prāṇa, or Śakti, or Ananda. In the Tantras *Prāṇa* (the Vital Breath) is a principle inferior to Śakti (Will), in Vaiṣṇavism Śakti (Will) (the cosmic creative energy) is inferior to Bliss. Corresponding to these there are different forms of mystical expression; but the identical urge of transcending the mental valuations and formations is exhibited everywhere, for anyhow the mental is looked upon as a limited perspective. Naturally mysticism, especially dynamic mysticism, is bent upon assimilating the wider life, either in the submental or in the super-mental life. The Indian mysticism in pursuance of these demands has various expressions. There is a special difference in the form and style of approach but everywhere the incompatibilities of our nature are removed by an inflow from the cosmic depths either of the vital, or of the spiritual existence. The intimate acquaintance and contact with the harmony and poise and vital being, with the oscillations of the cosmic will and energy and with the rhythmic pulsation in Bliss introduces us into definite orders of expression with different felicities. The consuming force is not everywhere the same, though each gives freedom from the wonted ways of life.

Vaiṣṇavism conceives the basic reality to be *asthetico-dynamic*. The cosmic will is the same principle in relation to the creative order. Its creative aspect can only come out in relation to the world order, where some tension is experienced and this tension brings out the basic principle as the creative Will, but in the heart of reality there is no tension. It is essentially Bliss with its expression in beauty, grace, love, and knowledge. Vaiṣṇavic mysticism conceives the fulfilment of our being spiritual life. Here personality gets its finest expression and the resistance of the creative order is removed. In fact, personalism in religion conceives the highest expression of our being in knowledge, love, even in will, but Will here has its spontaneous expression in the ease and harmony of movement without the least resistance which it experiences in the creative order. This easy and graceful movement of our being in harmony and joy evidently without any purpose is what characterises the Vaiṣṇavic from of mysticism from the other form where the creative will and vitality get their expression. In the dynamic mysticism there is an effort to identify our will the cosmic will in order that the finite will may move with the strength and surety of the cosmic will; but this is really a movement in the world of finite purposes and events. This cannot aspire to rise above the creative will and express the blissful movements in the world of spirits. Because of these limitations, Vaiṣṇavism does not favour the magnitude and development of will. The creative dynamism in it is replaced by aesthetic dynamism. The world of creative realms or ends is replaced by the kingdom of spirit. Will becomes the spontaneous expression of Bliss. However, Vaiṣṇavism does not ignore any side of our nature; in the mystical development, the intellect, aesthetic sensibility and love find their complete expression. They are the three anagogic faculties. "They are apt to flow over," as Inge says "into each other."

CHAPTER-III

Philosophical Mysticism

Philosophy, following the lead of the Vedāntic inspiration, has given two fundamentally different forms of Mysticism (1) Dynamical, and (2) Transcendental. The one is characterised by the emphasis on the dynamical character of knowledge and consciouness, the other, by its transcendental character. Transcendental mysticism accepts the Absolute as the fundamental philosophic concept, and the right mystical objective is an end in which the distinction between the finite self and the Absolute is lost. The finite self is absolved from the intricate mazes of life and is installed in the consciousness of freedom which is its essence and nature. This emphasis on the Absolute Experience takes away the value of all other experiences, sensuous, aesthetic, moral and spiritual and finds an all-absorbing satisfaction in Transcendental Awareness. The negation of life and experience is what characterises this form of Absolutism, and naturally it cannot be long maintained in actual life, for it inspires a kind of negative attitude towards the creative values of life. This kind of thought reaches far beyond the diverse expressions of our composite nature into the deep abyss of being where-from the spiritual or psychic dynamism is completely dropped. The life of will and the life of faith serve end or purpose. They are active movements associated with the creative life. But the movement of the primal will and the movement of spirit have no definite end, the formations are beyond the creative plane. They serve no purpose save and except that they afford the highest expression of delight. Will and empirical faith are associated with creative formations, but the expressive formations have no place in the rarefied consciousness or transcendent awarness. Creative Life and Faith are associated intimately. Faith is the shaping and directing force. It is the guidence and movement of spirit. And as such there is the unconscious prompting in our being to be expressive or creative, expressive in actual life; and actuality is associated with creativity. Spirit is act. There is a school of thought which presents this truth and develops a philosophy and mysticism on this basis.

Though Vaiṣṇavism emphasises the devotional form of mysticism, it will be hardly correct to say that Vaiṣṇavism is exclusively that. In Vaiṣṇavism there are different shades of mysticism, which originate from the emphasis laid upon some phases of its expression rather than others. Vaiṣṇavism offers, along with others, philosophic mysticism. It arises from the thinking view of things. Here strees is laid upon the all-inclusive experience which arises from the fostering of a philosophic sense and intuition. Vaiṣṇavism has not denied to itself the synoptic vision of reality. Vaiṣṇavism gives a kind of concrete absolutism and exhibits a synthetic order of things, and in the highest intellectual reach the synthetic order becomes a matter or living realisation. There may be different in metaphysical details, but all agree that intellectual intuition presents the concrete and integral Absolute and gives the unitary vision of existence. Here the symphony of the whole, rather than the music of the parts, is what engrosses the seeking soul. There is a calm, repose of being attuned to an intellectual delight, because of the perception of all-inclusive existence. Our consciousness is freed from the ripple of shorter movements of emotional ecstasy and becomes responsive to wider feelings associated with the grasp of the cosmic and the supra-cosmic reaches of existence. Knowledge is wide and vast, feeling is deep. Really such realisations are super-conscious. They exhibit the total existence with all its wealth and richness followed by supreme felicity. This super-conscious realisation is more than an intellectual feeling or an emotional joy, as it proceeds from the 'deeps' of our being not always accessible. And naturally it is something that sees reality both horizontally and vertically in its height and extensity i.e., in its all comprehensiveness. Philosophical mysticism naturally follows conceptual reflection, because it is the fruit of metaphysical thinking. Metaphysical thinking engenders and follows supra-mentalised intuition. All Vaiṣṇavic teachers follows almost the same inspiration; though there are minor shades of difference in their logical scheme, their sympathy is almost the same, the appreciation of the total setting of existence in the Absolute. Rāmānuja, Mādhva, Vallabha, and Jīva Goswāmī, accept a spiritual realisation of integral existence. All emphasise the perception of the concrete Absolute which, inspite of its personality, embrances the total existence by its all-comprehensiveness. But here a distinct note is sounded by the Bengal school of Vaiṣṇavism. They are responsive to the different grades of the realisation of the Absolute from its undifferentiated homogeneity to its concrete unity. The other teachers do not show the same responsiveness to the progressive growth of the perception of the integral absolute. They do not feel the progressive movement of spirit from an apparent sameness to concretisation through the stages of differentiation. Spititual life encompasses a harmony of notes which develop out of a state of silence and repose in spiritual being. To follow this it is necessary to follow the nature of spiritual reality.

This is the classical line of thinking with the Vaiṣṇavas. The dynamism of life and spirit is affiliated by them to the absolute Reality. The Absolute is both being and becoming,—the one is not without the other. Spirit is essentially movement and creation.

This affiliation of becoming with being introduces a great change in the whole out-look of life and thought. Every movement becomes a pulse of the divine life. Life becomes a movement in divine beauty and significance, impregnated with divine wisdom and skill. In place of mute and dumb stillness, we are offered the synthetic being with oscillation of life and joy and luminous consciousness. The divine life is concrete life in its fullest sense and its richness is due to infinite possibilities integrated in perfect harmony.

The introduction of the dynamic nature into the Absolute calls for a great change in the whole view of life in its meaning and its spiritual objective. It admits a kind of aesthetico-teleological conception of reality, makes our knowledge and experience concrete in every stage and expression.

Reality is concrete, and this character it must possess whatever its field of expression may be. It is an existence which integrates all the forms of creative expression. It might have different grades of expression, but it is immanent in every order in varying degrees.

Matter, life and mind are all expressions of reality. It has expressions even beyond them in the subtler forms of existence and finally in the transcendent universe of spirit. To think matter alone, or life or mind along is to lose the integrative conception philosophically and to suffer spiritually. It gives the discrete view of things and cannot read the continuity that runs through them.

The mere sense of the whole is nothing if it is not worked out of its fullest extent through the concrete knowledge of the details. The graded orders of existence, matter, life, mind, spirit and the Absolute and their place in the realm of nature and in the realm of values may satisfy the philosophic intelligence. Philosophy contemplates the orders of relations, but cannot see the functioning of active spirit in them. The philosophic conception has still its value, for it makes the mind ready for the next stage of development and expression in mystical approach. Vaiṣṇavic mysticism follows Vaiṣṇavic thought which establishes an order of spirit interlocked in the concrete divine. The order of nature is an expression of the divine thought, and inanimate animate existence, but the order of spirit exhibits the higher order of the divine expression through free begins and intelligences. In the former there is movement, oscillation, change, but they are not organised enough to reflect consciousness. In the latter the free play of creative spirit and consciousness is quite evident. The Vaiṣṇavic teachers do not lend support to emergent evolution and do not trace the development of life or thought from the non-conscient or non-sentient primal existence. They accept the thread of continuity through all the grades of being, but in the order of existence mind, life and matter follow the line of descent. And it is very important to remember that the order of descent represents the expression of Reality through limitation and ignorance. Evolution is, therefore, more a downward than an upward movement. In Indian philosophy evolution almost everywhere has the same meaning, and here thinkers do not differ much. There is in the infinite a necessity of self-expression. Reality is self expression. This means concreteness but not limitation. Limitation appears when the process is singled out and the successive stages in the process demand exclusive attention. Differentiation takes place in the process, but reality as a whole is integral.

The Vaiṣṇavas take reality as whole and integral, yet

they keep the three orders of Nature, Spirit and God as elements of existence in the integrity of the concrete whole. As elements they have different characters and separative existence and therefore they have definite orders, a separate history and they exist in their partially positive character and values. But this sectional view of things is not philosophy, far less mysticism. The philosophic intuition sees integrative existence, the mystic intuition, the liveliness of the divine expression through all the stages.

What interests one in Vaiṣṇavism is that it views everything from the aspect of eternity, and places every element of existence in the divine setting. It does not withdraw reality from anything, it is not satisfied so long as things are not presented as moments in the divine existence. Hence there is the demand in Vaiṣṇavic mysticism to view not only the totality as divine, but to read and to see every moment in divine light. The dignity of dynamical mysticism lies there, for it is not content with the mere structural reality, but with necessity, importance, beauty and play of elements integrated in the super-structure. Vaiṣṇavism has accepted categories of existence as not only signifying constitutive moments of the whole, but as fulfilling a spiritual function and purpose. The true understanding is not only metaphysical but spiritual. The spiritual understanding surpasses the metaphysical. It exhibits a significance which is not contained in the metaphysical, the bearing of reality upon life. This is specially a spiritual problem, not merely an ethical one. It is the most fascinating aspect of Vaiṣṇavism. It reads the bearing of thought on life and has developed an esotericism in consonance with the unfolding of life in love and grace. Vaiṣṇavism as philosophy represents the synthetic character of thought and reality, and as mysticism it makes out the dynamical forces that are shaping the spiritual unfolding and aspiration. The forces have not much importance in the scheme of thought. In Vaiṣṇavism the spiritual understanding follows the metaphysical, for it does not run counter to the metaphysical. It draws out the attractiveness, the sweetness of spiritual life. It adds flesh to the bone, beauty to the figure. Vaiṣṇavic philosophy represents the ultimate reality in itself and in its relation to the order of space, time and nature and the realm of finite spirit. And the whole Vaiṣṇavic Mysticism becomes interesting becuase it exhibits the different forms of spiritual grace and spiritual felicities.

There have been in Indian thought various conceptions of spiritual reality. The fountain source of these conceptions is the Upaniṣads. Indian thinkers generally build up their systems on the Upaniṣadic conception of reality. Whatever theory they offer, they take pains to prove that it is developed out of the Upaniṣadic conception. Thought allegiance has been made to the Upaniṣads, all schools of thinkers have not the same view of spiritual reality. In Vaiṣṇavic literatures (specially in the Bhāgavat) efforts have been made to develop a synthesis of the spiritual experiences of the past and to remould the philosophic conception on a new constructive basis. Vaiṣṇavism offers a fine appreciation of all the kinds of mystical intuitions and spiritual realisations and fomulates a conception of being which would cover the spiritual experiences arrived at through the diverse channels of Jñāna, Yoga and Bhakti; knowledge, contemplation and devotion.

There are three terms which require explanation. These terms represent Reality in its different phases, *Brāhmaṇ, Paramātman*, and *Bhagavān*. Their import and significance should be fully understood before we can follow the import and the practice of Vaiṣṇavic Mysticism.

Brāhmaṇ is the basic concept of the Upaniṣads. The word literally means the vast, the great, but this does not make the significance clear. It, of course, implies unlimitedness, immeasurableness, but that is not enough to indicate its nature especially from the mystical view point. The Upaniṣads have all along maintained a gnostic existence behind the mutations of phenomena and this has been called the reality. It is beyond all changes in space and time. It is the support of all existence. It is that state in consciousness in which there is no fleeting change of time—far above and far removed from our transient experiences.

In the mystical exaltation there is a natural tendency to transcend the finite experiences, for mysticism is the definite tendency to go beyond divided experience into the Unitive consciousness in which the soul gets its utmost expansion and is not touched by the mazes of phenomenal experience.

The Upaniṣadic spiritual philosophy encourages the widening of our consciousness, so that eventually in its utmost expansion no difference can be felt between the individual and the universal consciousness. *Tattwamasi* (Thou art that) expresses the final philosophic truth and the greatest spiritual experience in which finite experience and reality vanish into the Absolute. In the Upaniṣadas the finite distinctions are completely explained away, confining truth to the Absolute Intuition beyond the distinction of subject and predicate, self and non-self.

Brāhmaṇ represents such a reality. The search after the stillness of existence was so great in the Upaniṣads that all other values were considered insignificant in comparison with it. It resides in the hearts of things. When it is known, every-thing becomes known. The attraction of such a reality is so high, its realisation such a great possibility, that the soul pants after it and in its anxiety to get rid of the limitation of a divided existence, it sounds the death-knell in the emancipation of its individualistic and specialised consciousness. It is natural. The agony of existence is removed in the fuller and the completer consciousness. The throbbing self finds rest and peace when it is thus released from its enslaved state and bondage.

The Upaniṣads indicate suchness or thatness of existence. It can never be known, for it is the apex of consciousness beyond all differentiations, even beyond the bipolar relation of subject and object. Spiritual experience in its finest essence is an experience wherein time-sense is dropped and the soul is made free from the compelling sense and limitation of time. It is a time-free Experience. Accustomed as we are to associate our experience with time, it is difficult to conceive such a state or to call it experience. But our consciousness passes beyond all dimensions in its freedom from this restriction in mental expression through space and time.

The use of the term Brāhmaṇ in this meaning and connotation exactly has not been accepted by Vaiṣṇava schools. Rāmānuja fights out such conception of existence and intuition, for he believes the ultimate reality to be essentially dynamical and in the dynamical existence no state can be conceived which is a state of pure stillness or silence.

Intuition is essentially an act of spirit in which the object is reported to the subject, and the two seem to be interrelated in an organic relation. Knowledge is essentially an aesthetic or teleological process which grows in an organic way, and in no stage of knowledge this teleology exhibiting an internal relationship between the subject and the object can be conceived to be totally absent. Spiritual philosophy is interested in this organic expression of life and knowledge, for it ultimately leads on to the realisation of the unitive experience which represents the ultimate existence as a community of spirits. Rāmānuja could no-where see a better promise of spiritual life than in this experience; the divine life here is experienced as well-laid through all existence in its ever-increasing expression from the dumb mute nature to the older of angels and archangels. And the final beatitude consists in the realisation of the gross and the subtle existence moving in the harmoney of divine life and in the light of integral wisdom.

Rāmānuja exposes the futility of an experience beyond the functioning of the subject and the object. It gives according to him a barren philosophy and advances a fruitless spirituality. It neither inspires nor helps life, for the whole effort is negative and ends in a negation of life and experience. Spiritual life is essentially dynamical, and is attractive because of the richness of experience it affords. It is not contained in a barren awareness, but in the fine possibilities and fruitions that it promises. It is not the denial of life, it is rather enjoying its wide felicities and undreamt-of possibilities in the uprising of spirit. Vaiṣṇavism generally veers round this conception. Experience at no stage transcends its aestheticoteleological character, be it in usual experience or in spiritual experience. It can reach super-cosmic layers, still its fundamental character is not changed, and life everywhere is felt in reference to an 'other' though the other is integrated in the perception of the whole. Mystical experience is essentially concrete. The movements of life, mind and super-mind resemble in their concreteness, though in their fuller and finer development they represent the scale of ascendence. The higher scale focusses wider and more integrative movements. In mystical life these wider movements are directly revealed in their cosmic and super-cosmic expressions. The finite harmonies of existence from the lowest to the highest are felt and enjoyed. The details of existence together with their setting in the whole indicate the richness of experience.

Vaiṣṇavic teachers in Bengal like Rāmānuja believe in the dynamical nature of the ultimate reality and experience. But following the lead of inner experience they hold that spiritual differentiation follows the primordial spiritual sameness. This is, according to them, a definite stage, an initial stage of spiritual realisation. Before an integral conception in spirit could develop, it is necessary that the very basic foundation of experience and life in spirit should be understood and this requires a first-hand intuition of spirit as indeterminate existence. This indeterminateness does not deny but contains definiteness within. In order words, Bengal Vaiṣṇavism conceives a primordial spiritual reality, an a-conceptual one, an inexhaustible potentiality lying at the root of existence. It is one in which conceptual or logical distinctions are enfolded, but not clearly brought out. But none the less it has a transparent and lucent existence informing of its ultimate spiritual nature. No clear distinctions are found here. There is an unfettered existence, but no joy and sympathy of concrete life consequent upon integral and organic expressions. Reality has a primordial sameness and a creative potentiality.

It is primordial experience, in *Knowledge*, as well as in *Spirituality*. This is unique experience where determinations do not function. It is a state of illuminative silence. Experience and spirit have their poises and in the total setting such experience cannot be ignored. Whatever may be the philosophic significance of such a potentiality it has deep spiritual significance. It is really the first step in spiritual realisation. Life moves divided in ignorance, and it is essentially necessary to understand and realise that the movements of life are centred in knowledge and not in ignorance and this wisdom comes really when the initial back-ground is realised to be a spiritual potentiality fraught with immense possibilities. In life there is really a movement quite inward to pass into the primordial potentiality (absolute) in order that life can exhibit spirituality of its movements and functions. The consciousness of the basic reality is necessary to differentiate the movement of ignorance from the movement of spirit.

In this realisation the egoistic impulses and constructions born of ignorance are all shattered, for, an intimate acquaintance with this basic being requires a withdrawal and almost an absorption in the backgound. This makes us conscious of the nature of reality and enables us to see and read the movements in their spiritual perspective. The Vaiṣṇavas to build up a spiritual life feel the necessity of such a realisation. The fuller realisation comes when the basis becomes stable. It appears then that the spiritual realisation according to Rāmānuja is from the beginning a realisation in concreteness, fullness, harmony and integrity. The life of ignorance is the presentation of facts in their dividedness and multiplicity. Between the disordered ensemble of a life in ignorance and the ordered harmony of spiritual life, Rāmānuja can find no intermediary. Spiritual life is an order and a grouping of concrete experiences. The spiritual life begins when in place of heterogenous confusion, a harmony is established. But Jīva Goswāmī speaks of an initial experience of a wide homogenous expanse before our consciousness can pass to discover the richness of life in spirituality. Before the spiritual life can seriously begin, he thinks that there is need of such an experience—which inevitably precedes the concrete unfolding of spiritual life, for it indicates the emergence of a new vision and understanding, and a freedom from the life immersed in partial and half truths created by ignorance. The supra-cosmic reality in its apparent sameness and transcendence is presupposed in the definite formation. It is really the foundation of spiritual and concrete experience. Rāmānuja ignores this primordial sameness in experience and spirituality, for to him concreteness is the essence of spirit. Jīva Goswāmī introduces the note of poise in experience and spirituality, before they can pass into definite formations. The higher concreteness comes with definite foramtions and expressions, and includes and primordial potentiality as its incomplete and indefinite expression.

This realisation is not to be thought of merely in intellectual terms. This represents a stage in spiritual intuition where nothing is left besides a homogenous spiritual consciousness which is far beyond the concrete formations and expressions of life. It is a kind of overmental intuition in which the concrete functionings of the subject have been suspended. There is a complete equilibrium in our being.

The stage of this indefiniteness and equilibrium in being is followed by the stage of concretion. In the terminology of the Bengal Vaiṣṇavas the indefinite being is called 'Brāhmaṇ'. Brāhmaṇ is the basic reality transcending all concrete formations, Paramātman is the basic principle which controls and regulates concrete formations. The principle of individualation is Prakriti, Paramātman is the efficient cause of this formation. Vaiṣṇavism accepts this dualism of the Sāṃkhya, (matter and spirit) but modifies it by referring to Paramātman the capacity of formulating, controlling and regulating the scheme of evolution of the different orders of existence out of basic matter. This order of evolution is really the order or matter, life and mind. In Paramātman the primordial existence passes into concreteness, for it then manifests as the creative principle. The spiritual principle has reached a definitely higher state. It actualises itself in the concrete functioning of creating and governing the universe. When by an immanent necessity the ultimate reality express itself in difinite formations, it can exhibit itself as the *cosmic reality* embedded in creative formations, and as the supra-cosmic reality exhibiting its transcendent expressions in the realm of spirit. Both are definite expressions of spirit, the one stands in relation to the order of nature and values, the other stands in relation to the order of spirits superseding even the order of values in its orchestral harmony, ease and grace of movement. Paramātman is the cosmic reality exhibited through the creative order and the order of values.

Paramātman stands in twofold relation, viz. (1) to the order of creative expression and (2) to the realm of finite spirits.* The evolution of life and mind belongs to the creative order. In Vaiṣṇavic cosmology matter, life and mind differ by the gradual degrees of fineness that are reached in the scale of evolution. But a finer evolution is reached in the world of spirit, where the finite spirits become active and a new vista of evolution opens up. Spirit can be visibly active throgh the higher mental vehicle. It can be active as conscious principle immanent in creative expression and creative ideals. With the evolution of mind, a finer advance in the scale of being is reached, for here for the first time a new order of finer grwoth in ideals is attained which is not accessible within the bounds of life and matter. Mind is more elastic than life and here it can reflect the creative urge of spirit in a better sense than life. It creates ideal worlds, for with it not only finer sensibilities are developed, but also greater creative powers. The evolution of life and mind and the emergence of mind into social mind with its values,—social and moral and their regulation and setting in the harmony of

---

* Hindu Philosophy makes a distinction between *mind* and *Spirit*. Mind is an organ of intelligence and deliberation, spirit is the entity behind.

the creative order—are not spontaneous, but the downward movement of spirit in its concentrated expression. The degrees of concentration indicate the degrees of the descent. The order of descent are not separate from the basic reality; it is the creative spirit that takes on the formations, and at no stage, therefore, in the creative order, the order stands distinct from spirit. The degrees of condensation and diffusion indicate the degrees of spiritual expression. The two ends of extreme condensation in matter and finest diffusion in spirit are really spiritual movements, for there is no reality save and except spirit.

The conception of the Paramātman is not only a philosophic conception to establish order in creative world and in the realm of values. It implies a certain stage in the unfolding of mystical consciousness where the absolute Reality is apprehended in its concrete unity in the world of nature and the realm of values representing the definite movements of the concrete reality in its creative functioning and descent. It is a stage of concrete spiritual insight. It constitutes a stage of spiritual advance. Concreteness is the fullness of being, and naturally in the vision of the oversoul, philosophical mysticism note the expression of the initial potentiality into the forms of definite orders of existence and value. But the mystical vision is not confined to a particular line or rhythm of a definite order, it is not an absorbing identification with a special note of harmony; it rises to the height of experiencing the whole existence in its integral setting though here it is imperfect, for the supra-cosmic expressions are not revealed in this stage of experience. This experience is the changing impression of the over-soul immanent in the orders of nature and finite souls. Rāmānuja calls such expression as *Lila-Bibhuti*, the wideness of manifestation as exhibited through the creative order. It is not fully exhibited in the cosmic expression; there is still the supra-cosmic expression in the movement of spirit within itself apart from all reference to the creative order. This order in spiritual beatitude exhibits transcendent beauty and sublimity of spiritual life without any reference to the order of finite selves or nature. This is beyond the realm of grace, for grace is the reflection of a spiritual current on the finite order of souls and stands always in that reference. The law of the expression of spirit here has no resemblance to its expression in the creative order. It is in the utmost stretch of its free expression unfettered by the idea of a spiritual purpose in the creative order or of visiting and redeeming the souls. It is beyond the order of revelation which really belongs to the order of the over-soul. Revelation is the Word manifested to the finite spirit. It is transcendent completely, shining in its light and glory and stretching out its being far beyond the heavens of the angles and gods. This upward movement of being is fully represented in it, and it thus represents the better and fuller expression of the concrete absolute. In fact it is in the highest sense concrete, for it represents the highest synthesis of the lower orders of beings, the over-soul and the potential awareness. They are movements in the integral being, wherefrom they are regarded as its immanental incomplete expression, and naturally are to be transcended if the finest tremor in spirit is to be realised. The triple forms have a meaning only in reference to the orders of indefinite or definite expression of spirit, but since definite represents a higher stage, it is complete where the whole is reflected in the supra-cosmic, where in the definiteness of the stages is better brought out in the total setting. The first two movements of being get a greater significance in the light of the third, for they are then represented as the movements of the fuller reality seen only in partial reference.

They are thus embraced by it, though it always supersedes them. This super-soul is called Bhagavān in Vaiṣṇavic literature. Philosophic mysticism is completed when the Absolute is presented to us in its super-cosmic and cosmic richness. It is not only an understanding, but the opening of the stretches of existence, layers after layers—in their intensive depths as well as in their extensive vastness. No bit of existence is excluded from it, and attention is focussed upon its cosmic-pointedness. The whole is enjoyed in its rhythm, movement and setting. The super-cosmic expression is called in Rāmānuja *Nitya Bibhuti* (i.e. richness in expression exhibited not occasionally in cycles of creation, but always in the infinite existence). When the mystical experience reaches such a plane, it can well apprehend the grades of expression of infinite life together with its total setting—the view of the whole is never lost sight of, for the creative or the expressive stretches of being however glorious and brilliant do not represent the absolute without the focal reference to the integrative centre. Naturally philosophic mysticism in Vaiṣṇavism is not the sense of exaltation or rapport because of a sudden movement and expression in spirit in its superior height; it is the calm delight which flows from the quiet repose of being necessary to enjoy the concrete expression of spirit in its integral setting. It is the opening of consciousness in wideness and vastness. Vaiṣṇavism does not seek annihilation or the denial of life but the breaking down of the barriers which constitute separate existence. The integral realisation denies separateness and presents the Reality in its full setting,—in its essence and in the glories.

CHAPTER-IV

Ethical and Moral Mysticism

The emphasis on philosophical mysticism is somewhat released when the sectional movements are set before us, and Vaiṣṇavism is interested in exhibiting the movement of spirit in its infinite variations through the universe of graded values. The study of these variations is indeed interesting, for it lifts the veil from the formations of spirit in different planes of its expressions. The life in spirit opens with the understanding and the realisation of personality, and personality is nowhere better expressed than in the moral order. It is then a creative agent seeking the assimilation of moral values and expressions of a moral agent. The conservation of values is the essence of religion; in the order of values the expression and the movement of spirit are definite in the formation of moral ends. The moral order is an eternal order, it exhibits the order of personality in its finest expression. Personality emerges in its best when it strives after the moral ends. There it is represented as assimilating righteousness and holiness. The moral order rises from the recognition of merits, the fruits of Karma, and the adjustments of happiness and opportunities to the eternal order of righteousness and holiness. Whatever may be the expression of moral life—be it the appropriation of happiness or the conservation of values, ethical mysticism takes its stand on the revelation of a superior person, the God of righteousness, the Lord of justice regulating the order of *Karma* according to a pre-established harmony and a supreme Puissance of existence, the expression of the hightest Bonitas. From the ethical-spiritual point of view, God, as the object of faith and distributor of justice means 'the principle of the conservation of values through-out all oscillations and struggles, or if we like to call it so, the principle of fidelity in existence'.* The law of Karma is really the manifest indication of the conservation of values, in as much as it maintains the unredeemable relations between our sincere efforts and sure realisation.

The order of values essentially implies the order of free creative spirits. The inter-relation of spirits to themselves and to the physical world is possible because of a pre-established harmony. This pre-established harmony extends to the moral order. Every free spirit meets its desert according to its Karma. Here is exhibited the omnipotence of the divine; power regulates the physical laws as well as the moral laws. In the moral order He is represented as the principle of righteousness and justice. This order of values really presents a free order of spirits set in moral and spiritual evolution by controlling the life of desires and affiliating the life of spirit. But the complete spiritual evolution is not possible so long as the vital demands are active. Hence it suffers a limitation in this that it still moves in the realm of nature, for desires represent the demand of the instinctive life more than the urges and indications of spirit and therefore the free spirits become subject to the law of Karma. The world of values here is pseudo-spiritual; value here is essentially the egoistic insistences and is confined to the satisfaction of them. The evolution of spiritual values is not possible so long as the spirits are not free from vital insistences; and the law of retribution governs the evolution up to this limit; for retribution meets the souls when they are guided by desires and not impelled by spirit. It is active as a check upon the vital being. Duty is not transformed into worship for the movement of life is still egocentric.

---

* Philosophy of Religion by Hoffding, Page 134.

Even in this order a finer evolution of souls has been conceived by controlling nature and by assimilating finer powers, by a greater opening in spirit to overcome the sense of agency. The sense of agency is not native to the soul or spirit; it is grafted upon it by nature; and by dissociation from it the yearning soul can obtain mastery over it and move in cosmic spirit. This a really a king of freedom over nature and this can be obtained by a complere indifference to the vital movements. The cosmic movements imply a mastery over nature. It is granted alone to us by Paramātman when we leave our ego-sense and its consideration and rear up an identity (however partial) of being with the over-soul. It implies a relaxation of our being and a widening of consciousness. It should be remembered that, though the Vaiṣṇavas conceive the atomicity of the soul, they accept its power of infinite elastically, especially when it gets inspiration from the over-soul.

The evolution of the soul in this plane is confined to the subtle movements of our being in response to the finer cosmic currents regulating the universe. Such souls become really helpful in initiating new movements of thought and spirit; their privilege lies in transcending the limitation of human thought and in successfully acquiring a conquest over nature. Personality in us functions under limitations and we are hedged in by all kinds of considerations arising from such limitations. When the finer aspect of nature becomes active in us, the soul works no longer in limitation. The finer being is more plastic, transparent and responsive to the cosmic forces. When the adept has the finer consciousness dawned upon him, he becomes an instrument to them. This would imply that such an aspiring soul would be acquainted with the cosmic laws; the divine dispensation would enable him to go deeper into the mysteries in a way which would produce more effective results. This superior power together with the superior knowledge would really make the adept's conduct and behaviour somewhat incalculable to us. But this is no mystery. It is only working with the fine laws of nature. Hindu mysticism conceives the possibility of working on higher planes of existence. We get an access into the higher plane and influence the functioning in the lower plane. This would appear as a miracle. But there is no miracle in nature; only that we do not know the nature and the functioning of the higher laws.

In this movement there is the aspiration for integrating subtle cosmic powers. Such powers and privileges indicate great advance in the free movement of our being and its control over nature, still it must be remembered that our movement is not yet completely spiritual. Though it is stirred by the deeper urges to meet cosmic purposes, still the spiritual life functions here in response to the creative necessities and is confined to them. It has not its integral expression in itself apart from all purposes, personal or cosmic. Indeed, the cosmic creative impulse is distinct from the shorter movements and has its beauty. It manifests the secrets of the cosmic life in creation, though here the spritual expression is fettered and incomplete because of a definite purpose. It does not show the charms of its expression unfettered by purpose.

Vaiṣṇavism draws a distinction between the government of the universe and the free order of spirits. The creative order, however finely adjusted, suffers a limitation. It is an order of expression of spirit through the instrumentality of matter, and in no stage of our development and progress in this order can be soul be completely dissociated from the touch of matter. It may acquire powers, it may have subtler movements, but still its function and formations cannot be completely spiritual. The unearthing of the finer worlds is indeed a higher privilege, but the soul cannot even in this higher and subtler movements shake off the dust of the earth.

The moral setting of life associates the creative order with the divine as the Lord of justice and distributor of rewards and punishments. It emerges as the supreme righteousness, and as the supreme holy. This conception of supreme holiness elevates our moral sense to a higher plane, where the idea of the good is impressed upon it. A sense of the numen possesses us releasing us from the life of desires and actions and giving the sense of Holiness. The sense of holiness is a unique feeling associated with the divine life, it is more than what is ordinarily conveyed in self-perfection. It is the spirit of the Good, which is revealed at the height of moral perception. It is not acquisition, it is a gift to the rare soul. This is the highest value that moral life can achieve. This order of value is fully expressed when our being has no earthly demand, even when that demand is for a cosmic purpose. The good that is revealed through the cosmic purpose is qualified by the particular circumstances it has to meet. It is to be qualified by the conditions prevalent on earth. Ethical mysticism at this stage is the assimilation of a cosmic ideal and guidance by its stirring force; but the forces that are represented in it emerge from the supra-mental plane of existence i.e. from Paramātman, for it is directly the formative force there. Paramātman inspires exalted movements in history and inspires persons to usher in a new cycle of civilisation. It ultimately represents the moral order and focusses the moral value. It inspires moral personalities to a new order of expression. The great spiritual personalities really move under such inspiration; they are moved by the urges that require expression for ushering in a new order of values and spirituality.

CHAPTER -V

Psychism and Supra-psychism in Vaiṣṇavism

It is well however to remember that the Vaiṣṇavas accept a kind of dualistic hypothesis, matter and finite spirit, both related to the divine, matter indirectly, spirit directly. What is more important from the mystical view-point is to know the finer expressions of matter. Indeed the Vaiṣṇavas never accept the existence of matter in the ordinary sense of the term. Matter, life and mind are really sets of vibrations—the order and definiteness in vibrations determine their nature. Mind is more transparent in being and more definite in its functioning. All its functionings are highly delicate. Life is more restricted in its expressions and activity than mind. Matter is suspended activity, because of the dominance of the tamas. The Indian psychologist characterises mind as the finest evolution in the creative order in as much as it can reflect the working of spirit, but the normal mentation should not be supposed to be functionings of spirit. They can reflect spirit in a limited sense, but their function, however subtle, is not to be interpreted as spiritual activity. In the order of evolution the mental intuitions, functions and scaffoldings are to be completely transcended, before the expression and the formation of spirit can be exactly followed and understood. Spirit is something totally different from all these, though the creative energy cannot work without the guidance of spirit. Vaiṣṇavas accept a physical and a psychic order. The psychic is a higher principle more potent with the spiritual force than life and matter. It is ethereal and is in direct contact with spirit. It is the medium of transmission of spirit. The detailed working of the psychic is difficult to understand, for it represents a subtle force. Perhaps a helpful explanation is offered in Sir Oliver Lodge's etheric intermediary between spirit and matter. Sir Oliver says 'As a speculative surmise I hold that the idealistic and essentially real permanent part of ourselves is in continual touch with this semi-ethereal mechanism, if so can it be called, and is the means whereby even the simplest spontaneous actions are accomplished.' It will be the height of indiscreation to think that the psychic represents the spirit. It is the medium through which spirit can impress itself. The psychic is the finest modification of matter, delicate and sensitive enough to reflect the radiations of spirit. Sir Oliver says, 'The psychical body is made of matter and used by soul.' St. Paul speaks of the spiritual body—he perhaps did not mean by it a body made of spirit but one that served the needs of spirit. The psychic receives the spiritual force and communicates it to matter, and under its intense magnetic vibrations, it can make the body susceptible enough to receive the waves that are communicated to it. The mystics are wonderfully sensitive, they are responsive to finer currents of ethereal forces. Indeed they are delicate spiritual instruments, because the psyche is consciously active in them. With the appearence of the psyche to the forefront a new order of luminous experience is revealed which is otherwise inaccessible to the finest imagination. The ingress of spirit into mind, life and matter is possible through the psychic; they represent the degrees of descent in the scale of existence. Of course in the ancient literature matter and spirit are represented as different orders. The Vaiṣṇavic teachers never deny the possibility of spirit reacting upon matter, though they do not give up the idea of matter as a distinct existence dependent upon the supreme existence. The idea of separateness is not complete when it is affirmed that the modification of matter is done under the influence of spirit. It is better to say that spirit in its descending degrees of concentration is mind, life and matter. This does not indeed dispense with all the difficulties of the problem of mind and matter and their interaction, but this allows at a certain stage of spiritual development the removal of inelasticity from the body under the force and pressure of spirit. Spiritual life in a certain phase is conquest over the limitations of matter.

This inference is forced upon us if it is remembered that Rāmānuja mentions the existence of *Suddha Sattwa*. It is the intermediary between spirit and matter. It has not the inertia of the latter, it has the transparence of the former. It is a kind of luminous substance, finer than mental substance and better fitted to serve as the instrumentality spirit. Jīva Goswāmī conceive the direct influence of spirit upon matter. He accepts transmutation in the creative order through the formative force of spirit. There is an influx of spirit in creation.

The spiritual adepts by the help of this psychic opening can really be more effective in their activities, for they have a wide elasticity in their psychic being. The nature of their cosmic activity cannot be fully understood from the mental plane; and the limitations of mental functionings are not active there, and therefore the freedom and the ease of the adepts' movement can be hardly understood in the terms of mind. Their activities appear incalculable. The psychic order is a luminous order of being with delicay and intensity of movement of the etheric substance.

The psychicisation of our being is a necessary development before we can hope to feel spiritual movements. The psychic being helps the spirit to react upon and influence matter. The psychic intuition allows the adepts to understood better the cosmic functioning of spirit. A new chapter of direct knowledge of the facts of existence still inaccessible will be revealed when the access into the psychic will be spontaneous. Freedom from mental limitations will be natural. Life will oscillate with fine vibrations, knowledge will be increasingly intuitive, and being will enjoy suppleness and plasticity.

When the Vaiṣṇavas speak of the spirit-body, they really mean what they say. The psychic body is the etheric medium. The etheric medium is a constant associate of spirit so long as it is active in the realm of nature. The spirit-body has no touch with matter though it has touch with the psychic body. The thread of connexion between the spirit-body and the etheric body may be cut, and the spirit-body may act in itself, independent of the etheric body. The etheric body is necessary for its earthly expressions. The spirit-body is especially maintained by the Bengal Vaiṣṇavas. It is better to call it spirit-form.

Spirit is, to the Vaiṣṇavas, essentially concrete. The spirit-form is then really spirit with concrete functioning in concrete form. Spirit-from introduces to the realm of pure spirit detatched from the realm of nature and its graded universes. These spiritual entities are not possessed of psychical or etheric coverings.

There are spirits which have psychic fineness and can move freely in the subtle plants of existence. There are others which are earth-bound, they cannot function in their etheric or psychic body.

The vaiṣṇavas suggest the following orders :—

(1) An order of pure transcendantal spirits. (2) An order in which the psychic being is receptive to them and is in

touch with them. (3) An order in which the psychic body is not developed to receive the intimations of spirit. The knowledge of and acquaintance with the psychic body is imperatively necessary as a condition of further development in spiritual evolution. It indicates the new birth of man. When the psychic comes to the fore-front, the *initiate* is filled with hope and joy. Wider stretches of being and perfection becomes revealed to him. Our being becomes supermely delicate recording the ingress of light, love, beauty and power. The psychic opening gives sure promise of spiritual unfoldment and reflects its incalculable possibilits. When the psychicisation becomes complete, the fruition of concrete spirituality is immediate realisation, the whole being becomes overwhelmed with the mellifluous currents of divine aroma in love and beauty. When the psychic being is well established the spiritual unfolding becomes smooth and easy, its indications become the sure index of a higher evolution.[1]

This division does not correspond to the divisions of self-conscious or unconscious monads. In them there is perfect or imperfect organisation which reflects spirit fully or partially. In any case this reflection is never complete.

---

1. Unless the Soul receives the ingress of Suddha Sattwa, it cannot come in direct touch with transcendent spirituality, which suffers in finest expression in the immanent order.

   The Upaniṣads give a better guidence. The Taittiriya Upaniṣat says that Ātman is enfolded by the koṣas, the Bliss-body, the intelligence-body, the mental-body, the vital-body and the physical-body. Beyond all these koṣas is the spirit-monad or spirit substance. As soon as the soul rises above the creative dynamism, it is made free of the koṣas developed out of the orginal substance; but it has still the expression through the Suddha Sattwa, the substance of the spiritual order, luminous and expressive and not fettered in its expression. Naturally in this the spirit enjoys the transcendent order of exstence and is no longer screened in its being by the koṣas.

Fine reflection requires a fine adjustment and greater receptivity; it becomes possible when the limits of self-consciousness are passed over in super-consciousness. The transition to the super-consciousness is rendered easy when the psychic being seems active, allowing it intimation of spirit in its higher reaches. The super-conscious differs from the self-conscious in receiving the finer and the subtle impressions of the spirit.

A distinction should be drawn here between philosophic knowledge and such super-conscious intuition (through the psychicisation of our being). In the synoptic vision of reality integral existence is presented to the adepts. Hindu Mysticism in its devotional aspects stresses this kind of intutive realisation. But it does not appear to emphasise it. It does not touch all the parts of our being. It inspires wisdom. But in personalistic mysticism love and service count more than wisdom. Hence the philosophic aspect of mysticism in Vaiṣṇavism has not been so much emphasised as its devotional aspect, where life comes into play and its movement become more graceful and beautiful. Devotion influnces life. Vaiṣṇavism has never lost sight of the joys of active service in love along with the philosophic contemplation. Life moves in its complete rhythm in philosophic contemplation and devotional fervour. Intuition perceives truths, but psychic intuition enjoys its beauty and adores it. Will moves in diving rhythm for finer adaptation in spirit. This movement of will and heart take place in super-conscious fineness, for there along, the finest spirit-movements in love and service are possible. Without the impress of the super-conscious the heart and the will cannot rise to their spiritual fineness. Their spiritual nature emerges when consciousness reaches its super-conscient nature.

Hence the followers of devotional mysticism have not

been satisfied with transcental wisdom. They are anxious to modify and transform our being, so as to make the finest movement in life possible. Here lies the importance of this kind of mysticism; really it is a transcendental knowledge with the wealth of wider reaches in transcendental feelings. Devotional mysticism gives fine promise of curing life of all its ills and making it fully beautiful here by establishing a conscious association with the source of life and by tapping a fresh draught from it. A rejuvenation takes place, a new pulsation of life fills us. The full charm and beauty are drawn out. The movement of life becomes finer and livelier, because life is relieved of its grossness and obstructions. By the spiritualisation of the entire movements of our being the mystical promise is completely realised here. Since the psyche is in direct touch with the order of spirit and its expression, it can reflect them from their heights. In any case spirit cannot react upon the lower order without the psychic medium. The psychic being of an inspired person is directly influenced, though the form of inspiration, its expression and purpose may be different. The inspired agencies have different orders.

The direct contact between the psychic and the spiritual makes it possible for spirit to exhibit its finer graces when the psychicisation has been complete. The psychicisation in itself is very definite advace, it acquaints us with the beauty and order in the setting of life, a beauty and an order greater and wider than mental harmoney and poise. The psychic reveals the vaster life with its intensive harmony, transparence and luminosity of being with cosmic vibrations and oscillations. This rhythmic setting introduces into the higher ascent of spirit, where the psychic oscillations are reinforced by the spiritual surpassing all possible expressions in dignity, beauty and rhythm of spirit through the psyche.

It is possible to enter into supra-mental and transcendent expression of reality when the subtle bond is established through the psychic. The psychic is the direct connection between the higher and the lower ranges of being. The supra-mental infuson fills us with cosmic inspirations and moves us to cosmic ends, because the supra-mental is directly connected with the cosmic. The spiritual formation under its inspiration cannot have that fineness and force which are exhibited when the inspiration is received from still greater heights of the super-cosmic or the transcendental. The direct ingress of the supra-cosmic into cosmic and the lower planes is, according to the Bengal Vaiṣṇavas, a rare event; for the cosmic purposes are met by the ingress of power and force from the supra-mental. The Vaiṣṇavic teachers have more or less the same opinion, for they view the ultimate reality as immanent in and transcending the cosmic events and purposes. Inspirations have, therefore, different expression according to the character and the height of the source. Even in the immanent order, there are different levels of existence and at times the inspiration may be filtered even to them. Their character will depend upon the nature of reaction and respone. In order to meet such exigencies, the Bengal school has given us grades of possessed souls.

Though the direct ingress of the supra-cosmic in the cosmic order is a far off divine event, it is not so in the case of individual aspirants. Love is the supre-cosmic spiritual force. When it emerges in its divine character, it can be instrumental to the direct divine contact and fellowship.

Love is centric in its function and naturally it releases its charge from all earthly attractions and carries it straight to the divine. Love functions spontaneously. It is pregnant with wisdom. It is wrong to associate it with vital urge or insistence. It is the urge of spirit to be expansive in being and knowledge and to be intensive in its movement. Love represents both. They represent Divine life either in its total setting or in its in exhaustible concrete expressions through the formations of life. Vaiṣṇavism notes the infinite tunes of life and cannot endorse the bare magnitude of existence without reference to the content in expression, in wisdom, in information, in beauty, in delicacies, in rhythms and subtle movements. The expression of life here is not the same as in the manifested orders; here the spiritual has the spontaneous and concrete expression in the triune form of consciousness, existence and delight. This is the spiritual life, the supernal light and the supernal delight.

Even at this height of existence the Vaiṣṇavas conceive the existence of forms and spiritual figures; concreteness of reality implies also the expression in *spiritual forms*, for the highest reality is the most concrete, and concreteness implies an integral existence with attributes and with forms. These are not mental or psychic forms; these are spiritual forms. The subtler life is full of subtler forms; and according to Vaiṣṇavas no stage of life and consciousness, except the primordial (in which they were not apparent), is divested of forms. Forms are not created, they are eternally there; they are not the patterns of creations; they exceed them and go beyond them. The creative forms are different from the spiritual forms. The later have no contact with the creative order.These are supernal.

Plato speaks of the archetypal forms. They are creative patterns.* Creative forms are active. They shape plastic matter and modify it into infinite varieties. Creation is really the process of grafting the forms upon the formless. Transcendent

---

* The sensible world is built up according to the Ideas which exist in the Mind of God; the ideas are the models according to which the Demiurge brought order into the world. (Inge—Plotinus, p. 51)

forms are purely spiritual. They are not in touch with the creative order. They express the infinite varieties that find expression in spirit. Spirit is infinitely rich in its expression and amongst others there is expression in form. Idee-force and Idee-forms are different from spirit-forms and forces.* The latter are too fine and delicate to bear the touch with crude matter.

Though the Vaiṣṇavas speak of spirit-forms they maintain their expansive and *embracive* character. The divine combines concreteness and expansiveness. The concrete form does not make it in any way limited or confined to a limited scope. The modulation of its being spreads everywhere in the infinite expanse of existence, though its condensed being always appears as a spiritual form. It encircles the whole existence by its infinite nature, though the infinitude is centred in a concrete form. The highest reality is the monad of monads, and it contain within it all the complexities. To possess form is not necessarily inconsistent with its infinitude. The finite is both concrete and abstract. It has infinite expansiveness in the sense of its overcoming influence and all-embraciveness in its organic unity and being. It can be concrete in the highest sense; there is, according to the Vaiṣṇavas, no reason why such a being be without form.

At this height of existence the psychic and the spiritual being come to the surface and a new order of existence is revealed. Ordinary human experience is far removed from this state and it naturally cannot see so far. When experience presents psychic and spirit forms, we are then introduced

---

* Ideas or concept emerge from the mental or intelligent order and not from the spiritual *order*. There is evidently a difference between this view of ideas and the view held by Plotinus. According to him "Each *idea* is spirit and spirit is the totality of Ideas. The kingdom of the Ideas is the true reality, the true beauty"(Inge—Plotinus, p. 57).

into a new order of subtle existence. Mysticism is not only a new knowledge, but a finer evolution in life. Knowledge can be vouchsafed unto us in auspicious mements, but unless life grows delicate and fine, it is difficult to make use of this knowledge and to make it permanent in life. Every step in advance is an introduction into the elastic nature of spirit which is concentrated in being, but enjoys the widest amplitude in its expression. The more our nature grows in delicacy, the more these two aspects of concentration and expansion of spirit become evident to us. Hence personality, understood in the ordinary sense, has not the same meaning in spiritual philosophy. It enjoys certain common qualities, but its finest trait,—the amplitude of consciousness,—is not revealed in normal experience. It is revealed in spiritual experience, where nothing remains hidden from the adept. This is really the charm of mystical consciousness, and espacially of Vaiṣṇavic mysticism, for it regards no phases of life as false or illusory. They are all divine expression. The divine life runs through the whole existence. It is not exhausted therein. Hence the spiritual realisation will endow us with the knowledge of every plane of existence and will acquaint us with its divine working. It will give us the knowledge of the divine federation of the worlds and will guide us through them to the realisation of the federation of spirits. The federation of spirits cannot be complete in the world, for the spiritual expression is here restricted, hence a necessity is felt for the realisation of the spiritual federation in the kingdom of spirits beyond the spiritual federation on earth. The cosmic federation is the reflection of the spiritual federation. It has different notes. But the finest note are expressed in the centre reflecting the life of the whole. At this point spiritual expression is most intensive and keen. Besides this, there are other centres. They are hierarchies of federations according to the capacity of receiving, radiating and reflecting the supreme spiritual current that flows from the central existence.

The divine life is not expressed in its fulness and completeness in the order of manifestation, for it suffers in its beauty because of its movement through matter; and the order of descent determines the crudeness of expression and the order of ascent carries us from the finer to the still finer expression of the divine life in the graded universes. In mysticism in general no importance is laid upon such subtler movements of spirits through the unseen and invisible realms of existence. But dynamic mysticism lifts the veil and reveals the functioning of spirit through the subtle universe. The ordinary tendency is either to enjoy the transcendental reaches of Being or to enjoy the immanence of spirit; but the definite functioning of spirit and its expression through the subtler planes is a quite interesting and enjoyable theme often neglected in the accounts of mysticism. Dante gives the pictures of such universes in his own way, so do the literatures in Vaiṣṇavism.

Vaiṣṇavism takes into account the psychic forces that are active beyond the subtle forces of nature that are determining the order, the beauty, the symmetry of life beyond the physical, the vital and the mental. The psychic opening reveals the subtler currents of the soul, delightful and radiant, soft and lustrous. They are to be distinguished from the intellectual intuitions by the sense of their concreteness, their delicate vibrations, their radiant forms. The psychic perceptions allow us a new range of visions, a wide opening which removes all staleness and stiffness of being and fills it with perfect grace and beauty. The opposition of nature is withdrawn and the spirit recalls itself in its freshness and harmony. Indeed it is the wideness and the richness pervading life that attract us at every step in Vaiṣṇavism. The psychic unfolding sees in nature's order something more than nature, the expression and felicity of spirit. The Vaiṣṇavas accept the immanence of God in creation. Nature has different strata of existence and the forces are active in each one of them. The Ahirbudanva Saṁhitā and the Nārada Pañcharātra have given the names of those forces and pointed out their locations. What is important for us to notice is that these force reflect the divine at the crucial point in nature, and as the evolutionary chain is traced higher and higher up the forces become more luminous, bright and shining. The finer forces reveal themselves with our spiritual aspiration and really become helpful this way. As the movement of our being rises in aspiration, the force shows the vastness of its field of activity, the subtle waves of life and draws us towards the realisation of the infinite range of existence with its ever-increasing fineness and subtlety. It is often wrongly thought that Vaiṣṇavism has not taken into consideration this cosmic experience and cosmic feelings as much as the intuitions of holiness, beauty, sacredness, and amour. There are spiritual realisations which are personal in nature and on which Vaiṣṇavism lays strees as revealing the most intensive delight and transparent bliss. But they do not take away the values of such cosmic experiences of life and wideness of being. It may be said that they suffer in the intensity of consciousness involved in supra-cosmic realisation, but they are rich in the experienes of wide harmony, vast life and expansive existence. These add to the infinite richness of spiritual life. Spiritual life is really an opening into the vastness and the intensiveness of life, it is a joy accompanied with the unfathomable magnitude as well as with the intensivenes of being. These are two experiences, equally attractive, but according to Vaiṣṇavism the later is fuller, richer and therefore better and higher, for here the infinite shades of feelings and experiences in connexion with the fuller life in personal relations come to the fore. The personal relations are most intimate and enjoyable, for here the spiritual life is expressed at its best and finest. Spirituality is essentially a personal matter, it is the finest expression of personality and therefore naturally it is keenly felt in its finest integrity when the personal feelings are most emphatically moved. A fine landscape is enjoyable, but not so keenly as the picture of Madonna. The highest spiritual experiences are personal; and personality in its essence and finest form is revealed in our supra-cosmic experience. Here it is not limited *in its expression,* though it is centred in a concrete reality. This unlmited range of its expression is missed in normal consciousness. This limitation is shaken off in its super-conscious height.

CHAPTER-VI

Personalistic Mysticism

Vaiṣṇavic Mysticism is Personalistic. It rises in the height of being, definiteness and wide expression as it grows in its essential nature. The shadowed personality is the concentration of being in creative descent of spirit. Vaiṣṇavic mysticism emphasises the richness of personal consciousness freed from its association with nature; thus freed, it enjoys greater possibilities in the supra-cosmic movement and expression. The other forms of mystical consciousness, either in the absolute repose and poise or in the cosmic vastness and movements, are inferior. They do not afford richness in intensiveness as well as vastness as personal mysticism does. Spirituality flowers in its finest form more in personal than in impersonal consciousness. Impersonal consciousness has a profundity, because of its detachment from false values and egoistic constructions. It is really a blessed privilege to stand as a witness to the privileges and possibilities of divided consciousness and to rise to a height of consciousness which is not perplexed by the vortex of contraditions. Its value has not been ignored by the Bengal Vaiṣṇavas, because it affords a relief from the stream of short experiences and is accessory to real personal spiritual experiences in their integrity, richness, cadence and supra-cosmic rhythms. Personal life, as ordinarily understood must any how be transcended in order that the true personality in us may be born and this requires us to deny the divided experiences and to find repose in wider stretches of impersonal consciousness. According to the Vaiṣṇavas, real personalism emerges after impersonal consciousness. It is beyond all egoistic or surface consciousness. The highest truth is personal. To be spiritual is to be personal and to be concrete. Vaiṣṇavas feel alike with Swendenberg in matters of spirit. It appears that they are influenced by the direct vision of the spirit-forms appearing before them in their super-conscious revealations. These spiritual appearances are not on the mental plane or higher mental plane. They descend from a far higher plane than the mental. The kingdom of spirits, which is Heaven according to Swendenberg, and *Vaikuṇṭha* according to the Vaiṣṇavas, is the highest point in the ascent of the soul linked up with the lower worlds, just as the highest point in the spiral is connected with the descending curbs. The graded universe only expresses the same reality with the difference in its immanental expression.

This realm of spiritual personalities is not apparent to many. The spiritual man sees the spiritual order, the earthly man sees the earthly order. It requires a decent burial of the natural man before the spiritual man can emerge to be responsive to subtler currents of the heavenly life and delight.

The movement of spirit is movement in Wisdom and Love. 'Wisdom is the understanding of divine things to which the spirit attains through Love.' The movement of spirit in wisdom gives quietus of being, the movement of spirit in love gives thrill and tremor of being. The wings of the one (love) flutter to carry it towards God, the wings of the other (wisdom) are tied fast by the sense of terror arising from the immensity of existence. Vaiṣṇavism prefers the one to the other. It rises to the height of realisation in personal consciousness and in the impress left upon it by the Divine Love.

One great feature in Vaiṣṇavic mysticism (this has been

especially emphasised in the Bengal devotional school) is the transformation of man into woman in order that aspiration, surrender and reception may be complete. This transformation is the transformation of spirit. Woman is the symbol of devotion, aspiration and surrender; the spirit of Woman does not suffer from hesitation and doubt, and by her self-denial can draw the influence of spirit and reflect it in her being. Vaiṣṇavism has insisted on this free and spontaneous assimilation and identification with spirit. Woman is the symbol of this free unfettered movement. By the negativity of her being it becomes easy to invite, receive and to retain the divine influence. Woman is the form of perfect dedication and intense aspiration. The highest in the divine can be drawn out when the soul approaches it in the spirit of the bride. Hence the emphasis has been laid on the doctrine the eternal Feminine in order that the supreme dedication may be possible. By the rejection of postivity and assertiveness, it is possible to grow in our spiritual being; its emergence then becomes easy. All spiritual systems have, therefore, recommended self-denial in order that the Light can safely reach. The Vaiṣṇavas, like Swendenberg, believe in the law of correspondence between Heaven and Earth. The law of correspondence teachers; as in Heaven, so on Earth. This correspondence theory attributes to the divine a form, and to the souls forms. The forms of the souls are female forms. In our ascent towards Heaven the soul passes through the process of complete transformation and eventually emerges in the form of *Eternal Woman*. That is its true nature in undeniable relation and fellowship with the *Eternal Male* in the Divine. This form is more exquisite than the angelic forms—luminous and radiant. It is the spirit-form revealed only in the higher stretches of Love-consciousness. There is nothing earthly about it. The Vaiṣṇavas place it beyond the realm of creative potencies. This is not easily accessible. Only the spiritually fit who has been able to evolve his luminous form in spirit can enjoy this rare possibility when the veil is lifted. There is mysterious connexion between the divine-form with the spirit-form of every soul, nay, of every thing existing and this bond constitutes in Swendenberg's words 'Arcanum Caelestium'. The spirit of God animates the whole creation arranged in an order of hierarchy and the force of the Supreme spirit reaches and extends to all the layers of existence in different degrees. The Divine saturates the order with its force, power, beauty, and radiance. It transforms the soul into the female spirit-form. There is a vast space, a celestial space, intervening between the creative orders and the heights of Heaven. The aspiring soul in its ascent encounters this empty expanse before it can receive directly from Arcanum Caelestium. Rest in the wideness and peace in this height often stop further pursuit. The sense of relief from the divided life is often the end of our spiritual quest, whereas further advance through the enveloping expanse reveals the active expression of spirit in its transcendental dignity, beauty, and cadence. The finest expression of life here in any plane of existence cannot be compared to this beatitude. The spirit can soar on its wing of Heavenly Love. "The inmost essence of man out of which the spiritual organism is formed," is unclouded by the least trace of attachment to the promise and delights of life in its cosmic expression. One who remains unaffected to the new turnings of life and the radiant forces that are released enters into the still higher spiritual privileges. The direct access is then attained into the spiritual heaven, where the immensity of existence is filled with serenity and sprightliness of spirit—a serenity and a peace beyond our understanding, a sprightliness superior to the most radiant expression of life conceivable in human imagination. It is possible to realise this when the hidden lustrous spirit-form in us becomes active.

This supreme puissance of existence forms its essence, ground, and root. It is easy to feel its contact if only our being would retire into the centre. There is eternal sympathy in our being for the divine, and if this sympathy becomes active, it is at once elevated to the plane whence it feels the direct touches, however entangled it may be by the extraneous forces. In our psychic and spiritual being this contact can be established, and when the psychic is to the front, there is the emergence of a new life in us. Spiritual intuition has this advantage that it can see and feel both sides of new existence in its supra-cosmic transcendence and in its working in the creative plane and intermediate in such a way that one can enjoy the upward reaches of spirit as well as its subtle functioning and movement in creation. In fact, it endows us with a being that can directly record the intimation of spirit. This indeed is the unique feature of Vaiṣṇavic mysticism that it traces the definite function of spirit through every movement of life, cosmic and supra-cosmic. This movement cannot be seen and enjoyed without the help of the psychic. When the psychic link is traced out, the divine oscillation is felt also in the creative order. The supra-mental and the infra-mental ways of existence are revealed to our psychic intuitions, for the psychic can cast its light upon the vital and the sub-vital as well as it can relate itself to the supra-mental existence. Of course it should acquire sufficient power and intensity for the purpose. The psychic draws out the divine aspect of things and beings and traces out the divine movements through them. When it emerges in its fullness, its transparence, luminosity, radiance, elasticity becomes apparent—a new universe is revealed where our psychic self can enjoy the divine expression, and through the intense force which it generates, the psychic reveals the spiritual-forms of the indiviual-souls, which then enjoy the concrete divine with its concrete expression. Vaiṣṇavism places great emphasis upon the concrete visions and introduces divine aestheticism.

CHAPTER-VII

Divine Aestheticism

A new conception of Aestheticism is the natural consequence of the transfiguration of spirit. The chief attraction of Vaiṣṇavic Mysticism is that it introduces us into a realm of sound, colour and form of spiritual sustance as distinguished from physical sound, colour and form. It explores the inner rhythms of things and beings. These rhythms indicate their divine formation. When the psychic insight becomes fully active, it exhibits a rare fineness and beauty, a structural harmony, a rhythm and a poise in their functioning. It reveals a fine aesthetic expression and an order of beauty in existence. A new beauty with its radiant expression is manifested when the forces woking behind are presented to our occult insight. The inward structure and beauty then are exhibited to us with exquisite harmony and absorbing radiance. All things and beings shed a radiance, they appear with the freshness of a dream, apparelled as they are in celestial light. Roseate hues, divine perfumes, stars of light, fill our being with the festivity of delight. They remove the torments of the soul, and place us in the realm of subtle sounds and colours, which is still beyond the reach of physical science. This divine setting of things finds the presence of divine beauty everywhere. The dullness, the coarseness and the crudeness of nature are removed. Divine aestheticism conceives divine order of things. Each thing enjoy a constant ingress from the centre of existence which supports it in beauty, fragrance and sweetness. The reflection suffers because of the medium through which it is reflected. The divine beauty has its own medium of reflection; it is a psychic substance (suddhā sattwa,) which exhibits divine beauty and order. Some would say that divine beauty is spiritual in its essence and expression and does not stand in need of a matter, psychic or otherwise, for its manifestation. Beauty is expression. And since the expression in the spirit is concord and harmony, devine aestheticism is expression which is perfectly harmonious and rhythmical. "Destructed" or obstructed expression is ugliness. The soul of beauty is exhibited in its completeness in the realm of spirit, for there is no matter to hinder its fullest expression. There is beauty in the vital and the physical order. It suffers in effect and intensity. Here the spirit of beauty finds resistance in its complete expression, because of the instrument or medium of expression. Hence it is necessary that the physical or the vital being should be affiliated to spirit to get a noble expression. The plasticity of the instrument will determine the degrees of expression, necessarily its beauty, in the creative order. Transcendental beauty is appreciated when the fineness of our being casts off the touch of matter; a spiritual susceptibility and sympathy give a glimpse of it; a transcendental seeing gives its adequate knowledge. Our whole being should be spiritually modulated in order to be able to receive directly the intimation of divine beauty and harmony.—"a scent, a music, and a blossoming, eternal, timeless, spaceless, without gyve, fair, fadeless, undiminished." A divine imagination is to be reared up to be correctly sensitive to the modulations of beauty. It is a universe of enrapturing colours, which the highest prism cannot reflect. The vibrations are so subtle and swift. Such beauty is realised in the soul, it is not visible to the eye. On rare occasions flashes from this height stream into our being.

Beauty has an indrawn absorbing power, and the aspiring soul, if it follows its gentle solicitations, can have easy access into the world of subtle colours and forms. The soft impress of beauty has the sure effect of uplifting the soul. It removes the stiffness and produces divine modulations of our being introducing what Plato calls "the Ideal Beauty".

In the terms of Plato (Symposium), "this beauty is ever-existent, uncreated and imperishable, knowing neither increase nor decay..." This ideal beauty participates through every form of beauty. "It is separate and self-existent, simple and everlasting, while all other beautiful objects participate therein, yet in such a manner that although beautiful particulars are generated and perish, the ideal beauty neither waxes nor wanes and changes in any way." According to the Vaiṣṇavic view, beauty is the divine essence which permeates the whole existence. It emanates from the Divine and permeates the entire manifestation. The beauty of the creative order, its harmony and symphony is reflection of the transcendental beauty, though the reflection varies in degree and intensity. Sree Krishna says in the Gītā (X. 41) "whatever is beautiful, understand thee, that to go forth from a fragment of my splendour."[1] The divine aroma pervades throughout, and in the creative order the divine is manifested as the beautiful—the essence taking the form

In Hindu thought the Self is bliss, it is loved for its sake, all else that is loved is loved for it. In Vaiṣṇavism the Divine is the supreme self, the fullest bliss. It is *rasa,* the nectar that please the senses, that feeds the spirit and delights the soul. Beauty expresses the whole being. Beautiful things participate in forms which comes from the spiritual world. We are reminded of the saying of Plato "the purified soul

---

1. Inge—Philosophy of Plotinus, p. 212.

becomes a form, a meaning wholly spiritual and incorporal; the true beauty of the soul is to be made like God :

Aesthetic mysticism is marked by its swift effect and sure power, for it has, more than any other form of mysticism, the greater absorbing power. It is characterised by its force of absorption and creativeness. Beauty resists the self-conscious detachment, which is generally pursued in philosophic and contemplative mysticism. In it the innermost life is bound up with strenuous thought as to the nature of the ultimate existence, and the delight if affords is the delight of calm contemplation and synthetic vision. It reflects the world picture, blotting out discordant and inharmonious notes and traits. In aestheticism the old experiences are temporarily removed from the conscious field without an effort of detachment. It sheds a new light on the whole experience, and moves to a new creation in blessed harmony. It reaches its consummation in the suspended expression of beauty and sweetness. This is followed by creative expression. There is no end to expression, especially in divine aestheticism, for here the spirit finds no obstruction to its creation. The attraction of aesthetic mysticism is essentially the delight of serene poise followed by the enlivening joy of a new creation. Doubt may be entertained as to the right application of the term 'mysticism' to such aesthetic exaltation, for the word is associated with the intimation of ultimate reality. Such objection loses its force in case where the ultimate reality is concrete Experience frequent with vibrative life and varied with its constant new presentations. Vaiṣṇavism invites this continuously uplifting Experience as constituting the real essence of mysticism and indicating its attractiveness. The joy of life with its infinite delicate expression, not other wise accessible, is the promise of the mystical life; but in this presentation of the oscillating life with the wealth of its enjoyment, Vaiṣṇavism does not forget or overstep the philosophic background. It affords such richness of enjoyment by providing sectional presentations; and in life's movement the sectional presentations assume importance. Great insistence is laid upon enjoying the divine life in its concrete formations, though in it the sense of the whole is shifted to the Back-ground. In Vaiṣṇavism aestheticism is characterised by intensiveness rather than by extensiveness. The qualitative variety has an integral expression composed of shorter beats and waves of psychic vibration calculated to confine attention to swift successions of rhythms. It naturally lacks in the vaster display of more exclusive type attended with more subdued joy but more pensive feeling.

The mystical life is an abiding concentration on the centre as well as the circumferance of existence, on the apex and the different turnings of life. It opens up the bliss body in us in order that a responsive reaction may be possible to the cosmic bliss. Our aesthetic intuition rises in soft lusture and ethereal delight when it encounters the ever luminous Bliss in the heart of creation. What Carlyle says of art as dis-imprisoned soul of fact is applicable to beauty. Beauty introduces to the essence of thing by discovering "the soul of fact."

CHAPTER-VIII

Activistic Mysticism[1]

Vaiṣṇavic Mysticism, though it emphasises the contemplative and the devotional approach in which the human soul has an upward aspiration and ascent and in which it enjoys the divine fellowship, and at times absorption in the beatitude of love, holds such a state is alternated by the release of energy which takes the form of service. Bergson tells us that contemplation generates exuberance of energy which subsequently finds expression in the form of service. The concentration on the summit of being starts creative activity and widens our sympathy. "Contemplation is activity which transcends the action which it directs. If the creative force remains in it self while it creates it must be contemplation,...creation is contemplation for it is the consummation of contemplation which remains contemplation and does nothing else but creates by virtue of being contemplation." It is a truth which devotional mysticism discovers and a delight which devotional mysticism affords us, for the outer movement now acquires a new significance. The movement is facilitated by the new sympathy, by the sense of identity with the whole which reflects the divine life in its cosmic manifestation. The sense of exhilaration and freshness, the increase in the stature of our being which are the happy consequences of mystical realisation never fail us and make

1. Inge—Philosophy of Plotinus, p. 174.

our activity more intensive in degree and more extensive in application. A new kind of joy is experienced, the delight of being instrumental to the divine service.

Activistic mysticism takes two forms :—(1) Service directly unto the Divine. This is indeed a transcendent possibility, which can be actualised when the spiritualisation of our being is complete. The spirit-form comes to the fore and strikes the chord of inspiration and enthusiasm, where the consciousness of seeking satisfaction of our being in divine union is followed by the new consciousness of giving satisfaction to the divine by ungrudging service. In this our whole being is concentrated upon the divine in a new way and new form. Here self-consciousness rises in its full intensity and the whole being moves under a divine impulse which is released after the identification in love. The identification in love is the concentration of consciousness, the movement of service is the diffusion of consciousness throughout the entire being. The one is evoked by the other, a high degree of intensive concentration is love is naturally followed by a graceful movement. In divine aestheticism absorption is followed by expression and rhythmic movement. Both are delightful. In spiritual life it is very important in as much as it modulates our whole being, mental, vital and physical in graceful expression. Service is worship and adoration through activity. The spiritual force filtrates through our entire being and spontaneously fills it with a spiritual cadence. Service is the highest possible art in which all the parts of our composite being move in harmony of spirit.

An additional privilege in the form of graceful movement of the whole being in adoration is wrought out in activistic mysticism. A high degree of consiousness is evidently enlivened with a high intensive spiritual fervour. The great advantage in activistic mysticism is that it gives a spiritual turn not only to our thought, but to our habits and instincts also. No doubt, where the being is already spiritualised, the activistic mysticism in the form of service brings the active spirituality into play and causes it to manifest itself in artistc expression. The spirit here manifiests itself both in *introverted* and *extroverted* forms. The extroverted is an expression in spiritual vigour and intensity. The reference is to the identical centre, the difference being only in the form of expression. In the introverted form, the unity is apparent, in the extroverted expression, the unity is not apparent, though the movement has no other reference but to the centre.

(2) Service rendered unto the Divine indirectly through the service of humanity. Our feeling and will acquire an expansive character after they have been inspired by the divine grace, so that their expression has a cosmical character. The range of our sympathy and service is widened. Nothing is removed from the horizon of our love, for the whole creation is seen in relation to the pivot of being. The sense of the divine federation actuates this high degree of extensive service spontaneously. No discordant note is raised, love keeps up its expansive force. The whole movement is joyous, and our activities are constantly reinforced from the spiritual fountain. A constant supply is kept up from the gushing source. Mysticism stresses this expansion of our being and our sympathy. In Vaiṣṇavism the force of expansion is found in spirit, for spirit has a vertical as well as a horizontal expression. Naturally the cosmical feelings are associated with the spiritual education of our being.

Vaiṣṇavism does not encourage *idiopathic* religiosity. It recognises universalism in spirituality. The sense of communism is never lost, and therefore the cosmical expression is only natural with it. It never loses sight of the integrative power of spirit. This strong sympathetic susceptibillity makes for the spiritual saturation of the whole society. Vaiṣṇavism favours collective more than individualistic spirituality. Even in the transcendent realisation, this communistic character of spirit is fully exhibited. No-where is the poise in spiritual expression lost; spiritual expression is movement in delicacy and swiftness though they may differ in intensity.

Nothing definitely can be said about the appropriation of inwardness and activism in spiritual life. This depends upon the kind of reaction that spirit generates in us; but there must not be the least doubt that the experiences are extremely delightful and everywhere the whole being is set to a tune, either of absorption or of expression. The form is different, the content is the divine joy in union or in service. There is a difference between expression in aestheticism and service. Self-consciousness is more apparent in the latter than in the former. Aestheticism is indeed a movement where in the consciousness of joy is more apparent than anything. This temporary lull and withdrawnness of aesthetic concentration in service is necessary to heighten and deepen the delight. Here the subject is never lost or missed. In the expression through service, self-consciousness is evenly raised at the high level. It is creative in the sense of producing a particular situation affecting the object. In the consciousness of service the object is taken under the care of the subject which renders ministration unto the object of adoration. In Vaiṣṇavic mysticism this sense finds delightful expression, for here alone the complete transfiguration of our impulses becomes possible. In spiritual activism our vital nature gets transfored, for here the spiritual consciousness finds expression through the movement of our being. The least clinging to self and its old inclination mark the expression of spirit, and naturally the active side of our nature is brought under spiritual influence in order that it may have easy, graceful and unselfish expression in the performance of cosmic ends. Other forms of mysticism also accept such cosmic expression, for the ascent towards Transcendence has the invarible effect of making our nature and being expansive, but here in Vaiṣṇavism the active service and the cosmical feeling have a special meaning in as much as they are looked upon as dignified spiritual expression. Spirit unfolds its cosmic play; the whole movement of life is spiritual not only at the root, but also in its flowering. When our service is consummated in spirit a freedom from the insurgent impulses and desires is achieved. Our motor being becomes the vehicle of the divine will in its effective expression. Will-lessness is what is realised in the intensity of concentration. Will-less bliss has been so much thought about as the objective in mystic life, that the transformation of our dynamic being has been neglected. This inwardness is really one phase of the fuller mystical consciousness. Its complete nature is revealed when the inwardness is followed by an outwardness through which spirit gets its effective expression in the order of spiritual, aesthetic and moral values. This creative impulse of spirit to give expression to the spiritual values and to establish an order of harmony illustrates active spirituality. The great gift of Vaiṣṇavism lies in making nature the vehicle of spirit and in over-ridding their conflict. This cannot be done unless there is a channel to discharge spiritual energy through the active side of our nature. The dynamism of nature is put under the dynamism of spirit. In the lives of the saints the conflict between nature and spirit is resolved in the transfiguration of instincts by dedicating them as offering to the Divine. When the Holy spirit makes its entrance the impulses are completely de-naturalised. This complete spiritualisation of being is the ideal which can be wrought when nature yields itself to the ways of the spirit. The recoil to the Holy spirit is followed by the sense of broadness and expansiveness indicative of the presence of the divine love in a heart seeking its manifestation through service. This wise identification of our being with the divine will be so complete that actually occasion will arise when the feeling will be evident that the divine energy impels our actions. Activistic mysticism is so attuned that the divine energy can spontaneously flow throughout our being. When the separateness of self will be withdrawn the dynamic identification will be complete, and the sense of divine possession taking hold of us will be evident. The individual seeker will then feel the height of his being in the Divine and feel directly his instrumentality in the divine work on earth. This is the consummation, the divine agency of the human spirit. The divine becomes the worker in man. The spiritual order reveals itself to the spiritual adept, and by being instrumental to spirit he establishes, this eternal order here on earth as it is in Heaven. This can be done by one who is conscious of the transcendent order and alive to the descending force of spirit to transform Earth into Heaven. This is the eternal call of spirit, and for this it finds its instrument in receptive souls whose nature is such as can easily transfer the spiritiual energy through its organism to the environment. Its formation in the beginning appears simple, but its momentous possibility is to make the adept actually possessed by the breath of the Holy spirit.

This form of activism presupposes renunciation of the usual ways of life. Renunciation in spiritual life has great value. It affords freedom from the natural ways of life, and it is only too true that spiritual life cannot be successfully developed unless they are removed or transformed. Renunciation is then natural as an instrument to the higher opening. It is really turning the wheel of life in a way in which it can manifest spiritual potentialities. It has a negative side. It rejects the wonted course of life. It has also a positive side. It prepares us for finer beginings. Renunciation is actually the rejection of the lower for the higher movement and formation. Activistic mysticism is a species of spiritual formation, possible alone for the souls which have set aside the natural ways of life. This is more than disinterested activity in which the self-stands detached as an agent remaining quite indifferent to the fruits of action. Still there is quick and sure movement with a new attachment to the divine. Between natural and divine attachment stands the action through disinterestedness.

Divine attachment is the indrawn urge of spirit. It is the spontaneous spiritual attraction which emerges when life has been freed from the conflicting and dividing impulses. It is an even and continuous God-ward bent of our being. Devotional mysticism presses more upon transformation or assimilation than upon rejection or indifference. Attachment is life-expression; instead of being rejected, it should be purified by psychic fire. Then instead of being a positive hindrance it becomes a helpful force. In Vaiṣṇavic mysticism the soul emerges in its blissful expression even in intensive activity, for it represents the one aspect of spiritual expression. Renunciation is the necessary intermediate stage, the stage of poise and inaction before the spirit can emerge in a new form of divine expression. The stoic indifference possesses the soul so long as the possibility of spiritual and divine life through action is not realised. There the soul cris out 'Now, art thou seen, O, Builder, never shalt again thou build house for me. My mind is set on the eternal extinguished is all desire.' This agony has no meaning where the soul rises out from the conflict of action and inaction in the harmony of life divine, and where action takes shape in the form of spiritual expression and spiritual movement. There is no illusion of the agency, the whole thing is just the flowing out of spirit in its graceful expression through service. The refusal to accept the dynamism of spirit as distinguished from the dynamism of mind and life creates this short-sightedness, and activities of all forms are supposed to be more or less mundane affairs which cannot touch the soul. The Vaiṣṇavas, in accepting the dynamism of spirit, make it easier to accept its spontaneous formations in all the grades of existence. These formations have no immediate purpose. Even in service they are a kind of expression of spirit.

CHAPTER-IX

Transfiguration

The Vaiṣṇavas speaks of the transcendence of the *guṇas,* but not in the sense in which the Advaitists speak of. The Advaitist sees the whole movement of life in the triple *guṇas,* and naturally he stands a witness to the whole movement of life as an indifferent on-looker, for his is the calm immortal gaze of the spirit, cool as the moon-light on a tropical lake. He stands a witness to the torrents and waves of life, unmoved in the least by surges. A trial of strength is between the supreme calm of being and the inviting solicitation of life. The Jñāni stands the perpetual witness and is not drawn unto the mazes of life. He is for the final plunge.

The Vaiṣṇava holds different views. He entertains the attitude of the witness in order to perceive and feel better the modulations of the divine life throughout the created order so that he may identify himself with the divine purpose and be instrumental to the divine scheme either in the creative or in the transcendent order. Knowledge is here followed by active expression either in service or in love. To him knowledge and life are eternally associated. To known is to act. Every fresh aquisition of knowledge makes the movement of life more graceful, for it reveals the love that is at the heart of existence; and the two axes of love are knowledge and service. Love is the essence of spirit, knowledge and service are its expression. Knowledge exhibits the underniable relations between man and God, Love, the eternal union, service, the varied expression in adoration and offering. The three exhibit the movements of spirit in its different forms.

Vaiṣṇavic Mysticism presents a fuller life-consciousness and exhibits the dynamism of spirit in the reaches of our being. It creates an atmosphere saturated with beauty, grace, joy, movement and delight. It is the exhibition of the life-force at its finest and best.

The greatest requirement of mysticism is the conformation of life to spirit. In the transcendental mysticism this aspect has been overlooked or shelved. All transcendental mystics have their final realisation in the oneness of consciousness. No doubt, in the scheme of discipline, they offer certain principles to regulate the native instincts and to bring them to bear upon the eternal quest of the soul by completely rejecting their solicitations and by rearing up a habit of discrimination and transcendence in thought which refuses them sanctions. Non-attachment and discrimination, producing an impersonal sense, can see through the values of life and produce the helpful movement of a withdrawl from all kinds of movement, including even the highest active expression and creative thought. A sense of repose in the silence of being is established and the highest value is associated with it in as much as it offers a new experience of freedom from the Life-impulse.

Vaiṣṇavism, instead of inviting the supreme transcendence in which the contact between spirit and life is totally disowned, accepts the conformation of life to spirit as the best solution of the problem. It has its uniqueness here, as it offers an original solution to this eternal problem. The transcendent spirit is associated with the life-impulse in its magnificent and decent expression. In order words, spirit and life-force are not two distinct existents. They differ not in essence, but only in the range and form of expression. Spirit in its descent in the creative order exhibits itself as life, and as such to our untrained eye, they appear as distinct moving always not in unision and harmony. In spiritual life this conflict is resolved, and life enjoys the highest harmony of spirit. The resolution of the conflict becomes possible not by denying life, but infusing into it the light of spirit—which removes the grossness of being and exhibits life in its finest manifestation. This infusion of spirit modifies the character of instincts. Instincts are nature's urges. They become spiritual urges by the descent of this force. Their crudeness is removed, and a total change takes place in our nature. The divine nativity is realised, and nature takes a different colouring.

Vaiṣṇavism introduces a new outlook of life and promises a new hope, a new joy in the re-formation and re-juvenation of life. This art of transfiguration is a great art. It fills our being with a new life-current moving with the freshness of spirit. The force is to be called down and the being is to be surrendered for transfiguration. A willing surrender and a helpful aspiration are imperatively necessary. The spirit of God works miraculously. It visits suddenly but works unfailingly. Such a transforming power has no place in philosophic mysticism, in as much as it is contemplation on the totality of existence which becomes possible by maintaining a conscious detachment. But in aesthetic mysticism poises in the different levels and heights of existence are experieced and maintained, and in the absorbing harmony the urge of new creation is released when the temporary lull in activity is withdrawn. There is a necessity in aesthetic life for an ideal creation; and this is hastened when new energy is released after a temporary lapse. Aesthetic life alternates between absorption and creation. Creation becomes better and more effective after absorption. Absorption enters into the heart of aesthetic reality which captivates our whole being, and the creative impulse is rainforced and gets its satifaction in the emergence of a new order of aesthetic expression and value. Aestheticism enjoys the total setting as well as forms new constructions—it is a process of becoming, and therefore, its joy is essentially the joy of a new moulding and creating either in the form of a totally new emergence or in the form of a new and improved grouping. Everywhere the divine attachment has been the basis and root of the spiritual flowering, for this attachment is really the force that carries us towards the centre. It is the spiritually gravitating force. This attachment takes different shapes in knowledge, devotion and service; every one of them is evoked by its subtle attraction. In knowldge it takes the form of divine curiosity. In devotion it is the integrating force. And in service, the will takes the shape of a cosmic force fulfilling the divine ends in creation. In rapport, there is the temporary loss of consciousness and movement in the stillness of divine union. Vaiṣṇavism generally comprises all the forms mentioned above, though special emphasis is laid upon particular forms as more convenient to particular temperaments. The ideal is to surrender all the aspects of our being and to approach the God-head through all the faculties, in order that knowledge, love and will may move in divine rhythm and act in perfect harmony. It is not possible to separate the one form of movement from the other. The whole of life is an internal movement in spirit. Mystical life takes specific expressions blended in the harmony of the whole. The individual notes contribute to the richness of the tune. The infinite life with all its modulations is never realised in the same scale of expression by every body. Our nature reveals sympathies for all kinds of expressions and becomes naturally affiliated to them. Some enjoy calm meditative joy, some rhythmic blissful expression in devotion, some outflowing love in service, some spiritual union (in Yoga).

Our whole being becomes saturated with divine force, grace and concord. It endows us with redeeming mercy. 'God energise as Mercy at the summit and perfection of his activity.' (Meister Eckhart). The highest harmony of spirit is there where the spirit of God fills us and redeems us from the mazes and entanglements of life. The best harmony of spirit is revealed when surrender is complete; and spirit of God fills the Soul in the silence of the heart. The finest secrets of spirit are super-natural. They cannot be given by the intellect or understanding—'It can never comprehend Him in the sea of his own unfathomable nature.' Knowledge must give way to grace. Surrender calls Grace into operation by establishing the finest divine harmony in our nature. The whole bent of spiritual life in Vaiṣṇavism is governed by the law of Harmony. Love represents its highest form, and in the forms of expressions, in knowledge or in activity, the spiritual life cannot forgo this law of harmony. Spirit is harmony in essence and form. Naturally when the spiritual life is at its best, harmony will be exhibited in all forms of movements, either of knowledge, love or service. Unless this harmony is established in our being, spiritual life is not possible. The whole secret and art there lie in finding the key to this universal harmony which is the law of spiritual being. Vaiṣṇavism gets this art in the Yoga of self-surrender, where the soul emerges in tune with the infinite. It removes immediately the incompatibility of our nature in the central core of our being. This direct contact influences all our movements in knowledge, love and activity. It establishes inner harmony and poise. Here the soul strikes a divine chord and therefore this harmony is more than intellectual poise or equilibrium.

Vaiṣṇavism conceives a spiritual kingdom in spiritual spece. No direct relation exists between Nature's kingdom and the kingdom of spirit but the spirit force controls and regulates nature's impellings and when it descends from a higher to a lower plane, transfiguration becomes easy. When the call is sincere, the spirit—force descends and helps the transfiguration; nature becomes refined and our being becomes the better vehicle of spiritual activity. When the vehicle is refined and the aspiration is sincere, the rare privilege of direct spiritual infusion is enjoyed. This really makes man a superman. There are exceptions where the divine for its cosmic purpose descends into agents and makes them the medium of its expression. Complete transfiguration is not possible without the direct ingress of spirit, and a higher evolution is made easy when the force shapes the medium and makes it luminous and transparent. Thus does it conceive the gradual assimilation of nature by spirit. When the assimilation becomes complete a new order in evolution become possible. The complete assimilation is not envisaged though it conceives the expression of spirit through psychic matter. Anyhow the Vaiṣṇavas exhibit a rare spiritual insight in which the opposition between life and spirit is removed not only at the high transcendent level but also in the order of manifestation. The process of transfiguration is gradual, it takes time—but it surely entertains the hope of establishing the kingdom of spirit on earth as it is in heaven. This is its hope and promise.

CHAPTER-X

Mysticism of Sound

For spiritual inception, Vaiṣṇavism prescribes psychic harmony to be established by sound currents. They can arouse aesthetic and spiritual feelings. The potency of sound to move the currents of spirit has been propounded on direct experience. Fine musical currents proceed from the different layers of our being. In Hindu mysticism sounds of different intensity and vibration have been located in the different parts of our psychic being. These sounds are associated with the scale of harmony and the grades of spiritual expression. Sound potencies have differences in their capacity. Some produce rich vital feelings and emotions. Some start higher knowledge, some awake supra-mental consciousness. The mystics claim that they have in them the capacity to reveal the hidden layers of our being and consciousness and to carry us to planes where sound emerging from cosmic consciouness can be directly felt. Our consciouness and being become elastic under its influence, and the unconscious in us is fully stirred. Sound-mysticism is indeed the great art of being acquainted with the vaster being and consciousness that enfolds us and of moving us in the wake of the cosmic life impulse.

There are sounds which affect our sensory being. There are sounds which affect our motor being. The former are pregnant with esoteric wisdom. The latter initiate spiritual movements. When the sound currents become imperiously active, they infuse into our being a new life, and wonderfully enough, it then becomes keenly awake to silence as well as to active expression and formations. The effect of the different kinds of sound upon our psychic being is a matter of direct experience, not unverified guess work. There are various kinds of poise in our being associated with the different kinds of sound-vibrations; they indicate the degrees of ascent in our psychic barometer indicating the richness of spiritual perceptions and the wealth of spiritual feelings. Their special office lies in revealing the graded heights of our being and throwing open the mysteries hidden in them. A subtler world with new spiritual vistas and raltions, a new world with gentle oscillations of life force are exhibited. One who is acquainted with the mystery of sound feels at ease in the different heights of existence. Veils and veils are withdrawn. New contacts of momentous significance are established in subtler plans of existence. Knowledge, Power, Delight follow spontaneously. At times, it is felt that the restrictions of our being and knowledge are uplifted and space and time limitations vanish. The whole of existence appears as a setting in the wide spiritual expanse unfettered by the limitations created by space and time. The Vaiṣṇavas, of course, do not conceive for a moment the absence of the active manifestation of spirit and naturally their mystical objective is to pass from the lasser harmony of the creative plane to the greater harmony of the non-creative plane. When the limitatiions of conscious life are withdrawn by the cosmic harmonies of sounds, the wider stretches of consciousness are revealed. Then the quickly vibrative consciousness sheds its unobstructed light. The luminous expanse of existence beyond the creative order is not before him. This expanse is filled up with delicate vibrations of spirit which cannot reach the restricted fields of mind or life. Sound elevates our consciousness to planes far above the mind and redeems us from its limited ways. It produces gentle vibrations which move the core of our being and reveals the different ranges of conscious life, far above the mind. The Vaiṣṇavas maintain that there are sounds which open our consciousness to the delicate urges of spirit, which are not accessible in any other way. The Vaiṣṇavas prefer sounds pregnant with such potencies than those which introduce us to spiritual calm. They think that the spiritual calm interposes between the creative order and transcendental expression of spirit. Anyhow such urges emanate from the depth of being, undisturbed by the oscillations of the surface consciousness.

CHAPTER-XI

Yoga Māyā

If surrender and aspiration give the spiritual momentum of our being, they are also instrumental in calling down the Holy spirit and making it active in us. In Vaiṣṇavic Mysticism the direct ingress of the divine power and mercy is not made at once possible; the Holy spirit forecasts its advent and prepares the surrounding for it. Yoga Māyā represents the Holy spirit. It is the principle of intermediation between the creative order and the Divine; it is the power of spirit which regulates the course of events in order that the divine may descend into cosmic order and direct the turn of cosmic events. Its existence is especially felt when a new spiritual expression is to take place and a spiritual order is to be established. The force becomes operative when God is to incarnate and to be active in cosmic affairs. The direct descent of God in person or through intermediaries requires a previous spiritual setting in a restricted, if not, on a wide scale. Yoga Māyā prepares this setting in a group of souls, so that when the descent takes place, there may be souls to understand and feel it and to be actively influenced by it. God vouchsafes Himself through Yoga Māyā in order that the soul can receive Him and enjoy everlasting beatitude. Yoga Māyā invests us with the power and felicity of the divine; it makes the soul shine in its instrinsic spirituality and excellence that it can receive the divine influence direct. Yoga Māyā determines the occasion for God's descent. There are occasions when the world order requires a visitation from the living God in order that a new cycle of spirituality can be ushered in. Yoga Māyā is the power that works to this end. It unfolds a new rhythm in the cosmic harmony. It determines the character and form of divine manifestion, accoridng to the particular requirements in a definite period of cosmic life and history.

It is instrumental in establishing individual and collective spirituality. The individual aspirant gets its illuminating direction and sure protection from Yoga Māyā, and sometimes it works as the inward urge for spiritual purpose. It becomes the shaping force that way. The Holy spirit sheds grace upon individual souls. It indeed takes charge of the aspirant souls and invests them with the divine spirit. The Vaiṣṇavas hold that without the intercession of Yoga Māyā, the spiritual life cannot get its true and concrete formation. More often its force works; but with inward aspiration, its presence and functioning grow clear. It breeds a new consciousness in us which reflects the spiritual sum. Yoga Māyā gives the divine setting in order that divinity might fully express itself. It invests us with Peace, Power and Holiness, enkindling the finest aspiration by eliminating earthly clinging.

It is especially necessary in preparing a special setting for the divine descent. It shapes groups of events in such a way that the intervention and interfusing of divine power may be possible for collective well-being. It heralds the drawn of an epoch in the expression of collective spirituality. A new world order with new meaning and life is established in which the collective spiritual sense becomes manifest. Such spirituality forms its nucleus round a centre which is directly possessed by the Holy spirit. No power of the soul can accomplish what Yoga Māyā can, for it is the uplifting power of the spirit. Yoga Māyā creates an atmosphere favourable to the direct ingress of the divine power, either in the individual or in Society. It is the communicative medium of the Divine spirit. It is through Yoga Māyā that the spiritual marriage takes place between the human soul and the Divine. Vaiṣṇavism contends that spiritual unfolding in the real sense cannot commence unless Yoga Māyā be active in the soul. Aspiration calls this force into active operation.

The definite shape, which the Divine descent will take in relation to the requirement of a particular epoch in history, is determined by Yoga Māyā. The force takes its individuality with reference to the need and time of its appearance. The power and the Holiness, the Beauty and the Grace of the spirit cannot be well understood and revealed unless Yoga Māyā unfolds the *new consciousness* in us. It is more than the finest imagination, it does not proceed from within. This new consciousness unfolds by the descent of a superior power. The supreme existence exhibits its divine splendour, its radiant beauty and throws out its soul-absorbing melodies in the *dance of delight (Rāsa-nṛtya)* through the instrumentality of Yoga Māyā. It exhibits the divine harmony, the divine fullness of life and its supreme control over the order of nature. For the aspiring soul it is the indrawing power which saturates the soul with divine inception. The holy spirit of God can make the invisible visible, make God assume human form that 'not only He might redeem men, but also that He might become visible.' (Swendenberg, The Christian Religion.)

CHAPTER-XII

The Eternal Kṛṣṇa

Kṛṣṇa is the central concept in Bengal Vaiṣṇavism. It is the supreme existence, the supreme puissance. Śaṁkara and Rāmānuja hold that Śrī Kṛṣṇa is the incarnation of Viṣṇu, the supreme head of the Trinity. Kṛṣṇa as a historical figure is a great teacher, an inspirer, and enchanter. He plays different roles. The historical Kṛṣṇa is an incarnate to initiate a new cycle of civilisation based on the divine gospel he gave. The historical Kṛṣṇa comples admiration for his wisdom, heroism and dynamic personality. Vaiṣṇavism (in Bengal) does not challenge the historicity of Śrī Kṛṣṇa, but it does not accept him as an incarnation of Viṣṇu; on the other hand, Viṣṇu is supposed to be the hypostasis of Kṛṣṇa. It is the supreme existence. Besides the expression in the creative order, the supreme existence has its transcendent concreteness. This concreteness is its own. Love is the supreme concrete existence. Kṛṣṇa is Love. Love is Kṛṣṇa. The eternal Kṛṣṇa is manifested in exquisite beauty and captivating form. It is the shekinah of the divine consciousness. It is the centre of spiritual effulgence and radiation. The form is spiritual. It emits light, fragrance, beauty and aroma. The soul, the mind and the sense, find their perennial joy and satisfaction in it. It starts divine rhythm of being which transports the soul and the senses. In this rhythm all aridities are removed from our being, and a concord is established in the whole texture of our being.

Vaiṣṇavism affords this possibility of enjoying the spiritual delight through its impress upon the whole existence through all the avenues of expression. Hence naturally, Vaiṣṇavism affords spiritual delight along with philosophic contemplation of reality and values. The one is spiritual life presented in its infinite intensive modulations, the other is the life in spirit presented in its wideness. Śri Kṛṣṇa evokes both these kinds of feelings according to the character of conception, a wide peace along with the quick dance of being. The mingling of wide being, intensive harmony and blessedness together with graceful movement is what characterises the spiritual felicitation in Vaiṣṇavism. Kṛṣṇa wakes up such modulations in our being and satisfies the demands of Love, Knowledge and Peace. Kṛṣṇa is all these in their integrative synthesis.

Kṛṣṇa is also the redeemer of souls. Kṛṣṇa is grace, Grace shows Him in relation to human souls and the world of spiritual values. Redemption is a spiritual act. It is associated with values. It is the ingress of the transcendent spirit into realm of values; naturally it meets here the experience of tension. The loving grace is at the root of incarnation in human form and shape. It is the connecting link between Heaven and Earth.

The eternal Kṛṣṇa is then the full God-Head in all His attributes. He naturally transcends the creative plane of existence, though his hypostasis are active there, and regulates the concrete events in obedience to the divine purpose. Caitanya propounds the conception of the Eternal Kṛṣṇa, as the supreme Love and the supreme Bliss. He is the divine bridegroom, to whom all the souls of Heaven and Earth are attached. He fills the whole of existence with the flood of harmony, and the aspiring souls move with it to realise the resonance in spirit. The finest music of life is felt deep within the recesses of being. A new order of life with its divine expression is revealed wherein life rises in its completest beatitude, richest harmonies, lustrous experiences, delicacies of movements and fullness of being.

The doctrine of the Eternal Kṛṣṇa gets its hold amongst the Vaiṣṇava Mystics, because of the fine rhythm and the delightful repose it awakes in our psychic being; and they claim that unless there is the delicate spiritual tuning of our being, the supra-mental harmonies which it evokes cannot be realised. All the higher currents of the soul, wisdom, love, bliss make their appearance when our being is transported by its subtle attractions. The Vaiṣṇava Mystics in Bengal see in Kṛṣṇa the source of all the wonders of spiritual life, which are actualised in living realisation when the consciousness is stirred up under its influence. The basis of mystical life rests on freedom, elasticity and harmony. The Vaiṣṇavas hold that the flute of Kṛṣṇa affords them all. These rich dynamic spiritual possibilities, which it wakes up have been an additional ground in favour of the doctrine of the eternal Kṛṣṇa.

Kṛṣṇa awakens spiritual harmonies in us; it is wrong to associate Him with the originator of vital impulse. The spiritual harmony may influence the vital harmony and produce a sense of freshness and vital elasticity but the serenity of spirit is never lost. A calm vital peace with exquisite and soft delight of spirit is often the realisation. Our being is infinitely modulated under the pressure of spirit, and delightful harmonies are released, but the harmonies evoked by Kṛṣṇa-consciouness are unique, as they originate from the highest pitch of life in spirit.

The spiritual force is delicate, but powerful. It affects and rejuvenates the whole being and introduces a joyousness into every part of our existence, the mental, the vital and the physical. It makes them alert and responsive. This happy consummation takes place when the mental being and the senses are chastened and their aridities removed. Unless the 'God' of spirit is purified and refined, the spirit of God or the spirit of Love does not enter into us with its full intensity and vigour. Love successfully vibrates the delicate medium with its influence and power.

The economy of spiritual life requires that there should be a *purgation*. The weakness of the lower part should be redressed. This purgation must be of the senses and the mind. 'For if the weakness of the lower part be not redressed, and if it have acquired no courage in God, in the sweet communion with Him subsequently enjoyed, nature would have been unprepared and without strength for the trails of this night.' St. John of the Cross speaks of the *Dark Night of the senses* where the soul is purified. It is the sensual purgation attained by subjecting the senses to the spirit. The Vaiṣṇavas accept such purification of the senses. The purification, instead of appearing as a bitter task imposed on the rebellious senses, soon appears as a joyful surprise, for the senses and the mind are affected agreeably, by the force and the power of spiritual harmony. The senses and the mind spontaneously give themselves up to the harmony of the spirit. The inevitable demand is to grow quick and sensitive in order that our being, mind and the senses may react to the symphonies of life. The spiritual life is a response to reality through the totality of our being.

St. John of the Cross speaks of another form of Dark-Night. This is the Dark-Night of contemplation. Its ultimate goal is union with God. The disproportion between the finite and the infinite is so enormous, that the 'mere comparison must have a crushing effect on the finite being.' The experience is like entering into a stupendous summit of being where most souls can not stay long. St. John says 'Every soul will have to pass through this experience, the minority already in this life. In the Dark-Night of contemplation, the vast majority on leaving this life, when they will suddenly find themselves encompassed by the infinite majesty and the power of the God-head. When the finite comes into contact with the infinite, it realises its nothingness; it is trumbled to the ground.' This is also a familiar experience in Vaiṣṇavism, when the soul crosses the line dividing creative and the transcendental planes of existence, where the vastness of the supreme existence cannot be equated by the aspiring soul. The majesty of being and the magnitude of power overwhelm it. This state soon passes away, giving way to the alluring beauties and harmonies of the Divine life. Vaiṣṇavism presents contraries of spiritual experience following from the many sided expressions of the divine reality, all finally harmonised in the eternal spiritual setting. The sense of majesty, power associated with the infinite magnitude of being, is one that meets us on the threshhold of spiritual experience and on this spiritual background can the softer beatitudes exhibit themselves.

Another form of Dark-Night is experienced when the soul passes through the sense of emptiness and separation, when the soul does not enjoy visitations from the living God and the heart is emptied of beatific experiences. There is the sense of loneliness, the sense of anguish born of separation. The Vaiṣṇavas speak of such Darkness of the soul, a shadow which suddenly emerges when the light of spirit is withdrawn. But such a state cannot be long continued. It is soon followed by the more intensive movement of spirit. It is a lull in the movement of spirit, so that it can make ideal creations. With the withdrawal of the love-object, memory makes ideal creation and projection, for Love can not long bear the sense of emptiness, and there is in it the native demand of associating itself with its object. And if if cannot actually fulfil this demand, it seeks the ideal fulfilment. The Dark-Night is one that follows this realisation. It is neither the Dark-Night of the senses, nor the Dark-Night of contemplation. There is a necessity for such a night. The spiritual consciousness continues when the vivid life of realisation is withdrawn. Really it fills up the vacuum of our being. The occasional gaps in actual realisation and fulfilment serve a spiritual economy, for they allow the spiritual force to penetrate our complete being and introduce such changes in it as can make the realisation evenly continuous. This is a tension in spiritual life. It has its use. It supplies the momentum for the exhibition of newer impulses and movements in Love.

CHAPTER-XIII

Time and Spiritual Life

One of the promises of mystical consciousness is time-transcendence. The past and the future are great barriers to our freedom. Though the continuity of evolution can forecast in the sensitive souls the course of the future,—the future involved in the present and the past,—yet as conscious life does not experience freedom from the compelling force of Time. Time becomes the medium of its creative expression. It is true of the moments of time, past, present and future, for they are the points of actualisation which create epochal history. This individuation of time is not to be thought of disparately—it brings out prominently the actual events and the process of actualisation. Creativity is the definite expression of potentiality. Definiteness has a temporal significance and character. This reference to definiteness, when carried to extreme, gives the momentary conception of Time ignoring its continuity and integrity.

Our mental habits are committed to the reading of events in the divided span of Time, and return to it even after the momentary lapse of the time-sense in concentration. Spirituality is the process of actualisation, in a definite sense, the span of its duration and extensiveness is unbounded. But the concretion is well-defined, since it is an assimilating process. The reference to a centre and to extensive assimilation is what gives uniqueness to mental life and allows it to form a society. It is indeed always a potential society. In spiritual life the focuss of assimilation grows and the centre enjoys assimilation with the cosmical process and reality.

Time has its individuality. In history the individuality of time is most marked. The grouping of a course of events marks out its prominence and individuality. Each moment has its uniqueness. The uniqueness brings out the creative individuality in the process of actualisation; but the process of assimilation works in the opposite direction, it gives us freedom from the creative individuality of moments to the cosmic sociality of Time in the undividedness of the past, present and future. Here indeed the time sense takes a new form, not in its succession, but in its continuous integration. The socialisation and the process are revealed at once, and the integrative sense of time is presented, allowing us a relaxation from the concretising process and enjoyment of the total grouping. This freedom from the momentary time-sense and the grasp of its sociality mark the dawn of mystical experience. Mysticism refuses time in its three dimensions, and reduces it to the sense of the eternal present. Mysticism builds up this new experience; it is a new unfolding of life transcending the time sense. It displaces the sense of succession by the sense of simultaneity. It sounds strange indeed that simultaneity displaces succession in our spiritual life. That indeed, is the promise of all forms of mysticism, for mysticism generates this unique experience by the growth of a deeper consciousness, where the sense of dividedness which screens the integral view of things is displaced and the mind works unfettered by the ordinary time-sense. Even the form of mysticism which allows spiritual elasticity and free expansion accepts Time-lessness in the sense of the transcendence of the triple movements of Time. It conceives duration without compelling division of the past and the future. The true time-sense is eternity and continuity, without the serial presentations of the moments. Mystical training develops the sense of eternity. With the disparate sense of time withdrawn we go beyond the creative order of actualities and grasp the eternal order of realities and essence. We enjoy the expanse of existence and freedom of movement, since we have to make no reference to spans of space and moments of time. Naturally Vaiṣṇavism conceives the eternal order of spirits an order in perfect harmony where in the individual spirits enjoy alike the modulations of the infinite life in unbounded space and undivided time. This is true of each individual spirit. It now becomes free of actualising process in the creative order and enjoys freedom without actualisation. Each centre acquires the psychic expanse immanent in its being and directly contacts the infinite life unfettered by time and space. It grows in the sense of vastness and in the sense of eternal harmony that prevails in the kingdom of spirit with the full freedom from creative individuality.

CHAPTER-XIV

Reciprocity in Spiritual Life

Spirit life is characterised by the two notes of harmony and freedom. The finer harmony gives the greater freedom. A free-spirit can alone enjoy the note of harmony. Spiritual realisation is possible in a society of spirits.

This law of reciprocity gives spiritual life its security, strength, joy and elevation. Personality can attain its expression in a society of persons. Each centre has its own note, each, its own expression. Each fulfils the other. Personality enjoys its full height and richness in a spiritual community through expressions in Love, Knowledge, Beauty, Freshness Holiness. Each is the sure fruit of an adventure in spiritual life. This sharing of spiritual notes in a community is not enough. There is the persistent demand to establish direct connexion with God, and through Him with the invisible orders of spirits. Spiritual life is the participation in the divine family. It makes our realisation most intensive and extensive. The kingdom of spirit comprises more than the community of human souls and finite spirits. The orders of angels and saints are still exterior to the innermost order of spirit. They live in the wake of and in touch with the divine life, but are not one with it. They are functionaries. They have duties relative to their position in the spiritual kingdom. But the deepest spiritual life is to be in active touch with the Divine, not in any way harnessed to any functions associated with the cosmic events. There is the spiritual life complete. It is released from all imperatives and responsibilities. There is joy and fulfilment in meeting responsibilities for they are ultimately duties done to God; still they suffer limitation of stations. Duty has inevitable reference to some unaccomplished process some realisation, some striving. A life complete in spirit gives complete freedom from the sense of responsibility, from the thought of 'ought.' Vaiṣṇavas say that the life in Love is beyond the imperatives of moral sense. It is a spontaneous stream of Love and Divine passion released from the hazards and conflicts of moral life.

Vaiṣṇavism classifies Devotion and Love as *Vaidhī* and *Rāgānugā*. The former is sanctioned, it originates from imperatives and implies a strain and conscious effort. The latter is the natural and spontaneous expression of Love. It originates from a finer attachment to the divine life. The sanction implied in the former is absent in the latter. The former is the fruit of training and culture, the latter is a free and natural expression. It is the easy expression of life fulfilled in Love. It is *hidden in life,* and when life expresses itself free from all conditions, moral and intellectual, its first expression emerges in the form of spontaneous love. Love is the last formation of life, and emerges out when it has its expression un-conditioned either by instincts or by intellect or by any former habits.

Sanctioned love is no Love. It is a training in love. It is conditioned by will and intellect. It, therefore, loses the zest of love. A conditioned existence is not consistent with life in spirit, which is free, spontaneous, and integral. A conditioned existence is determined, divided and is a reflection of reality through intellect and will. Spiritual life is spontaneous flowering. It is the flame of love in which all is consumed. It is an awareness that comes of itself and comes when the mechanical habits of intellectualised will cease. It emerges from depth of being, issuing forth like an absorbing flame. It is possible when life and mind are freed from the mechanism of habitual thinking and doing. Love in the usual sense is set in the mechanical process of emotion, and this is certainly true of the Love which is cultivated under sanction. Such a form of spiritual approach has small value, and more often under the pressure of customs and sanctions love dies out rather than thrives. Different is the case when love is automatic and spontaneous. Our whole being is focussed in it and rises above the patterns created by mind. It is the habit of the mind to create patterns ideologies and thus lose the grasp of the integral reality. The demand of the spirit is the awareness of this integral existence,which, it cannot achieve unless, it be freed from the mental-constructs. Life gest its finest expression in integral love. Integral love is integral awareness. It is released from the sense of 'ought'. This easy expression suffers spontaneous attachment. It is called 'Rāgānugā' (the literal meaning is that which follows from attachment). This attachment is the natural, unfettered expression of spirit. Life is creative as well as unitive. The unitive impulse is Love. The integral impulse cannot work out properly unless there is complete freedom from the wonted ways of sanctions, duties, thought-constructs, and a sympathetic awareness and identification with life.

In the integral awareness of love there are relations, but these relations are immediate. The immediacy of relations becomes evident when the mind is unconditioned and iife releases its psychic expression. Relations become mediate through the thinking mind. They are immediate in life's setting. So that when the mind is set free from the limiting conditions, there the relations are conceived as neither distant nor mediate. They are direct and immediate. They are the ways through which life takes its concrete expressions. They do not divide. The creative act is one single act covering up the whole process and definite expression. Love is one single expression and act, covering up all the relations and stages through which it is unfolded. Love cannot be intellectualised; the moment it is, it ceases to be love, In love there is consciring (knowing together) but this knowledge is *immediate* and not mediate. The supposition that there is some thing independent is a metal construct which creates a barrier between knowledge and its objects. Consciring impresses the immediacy of knowledge in its entire and complete setting. Love and its object are indissolubly one. The one ceases without the other. Love is the creative synthesis; at every step the object is assimilated in the creative expression of love. Knowledge is bliss-consciring. Love is being and beoming, eternally accomplished and accomplishing, a living process which survives immediate relations. They are again assimilated into its nature. This is the way with a living process and reality. This character of love is drawn out in its supreme expression in 'Rāgānugā.

CHAPTER-XV

Grace

Grace works to evoke the finest pulse of Love in us. Grace is the divine response to our call and solicitation. The form and the character of the response depend upon the nature of the call or the aspiration. Where the aspiration is for fulfilment Grace intervenes not as the force that bestows the best in Love, the fuller Life, the greater delight and the finer radiation of spirit. Grace, here, does not indicate the *saving* power. It indicates the *completing* power. Love and Grace are the two fundamental bases of spiritual life. Love gives the aspiration. Grace fulfils it. Grace is an outpouring of life to lift the aspirant soul.

Grace as the saving power implies a distance and a dissimilarity between the giver and the receiver. The one is perfect, the other imperfect. The one is redeemer, the other is redeemed. Love here has not its finest expression. Love denies distance, it excludes difference. It invites sameness. It does not think of redemption, it is affiliating and absorbing in its impulse. Redemption is its indirect fruit. Love reveals the reciprocity of relation between man and God. Man is as much a necessity to God as God to Man. Love refuses to be alone.

In the economy of spiritual life, Grace occupies a supreme place, in as much as it represents the uplifting force which makes steeper ascents easy. There are pitches in being which are otherwise inaccessible. The finite souls may be aspiring, and energising for the realisation of spiritual ends, but in the spiritual world the law of responsive reaction holds true—the call is answered, the aspiration is fulfilled. The aspirant and the surrendered soul receive help. Aspiration and Response are the momentum in the spiritual life from opposite directions. Eventually the two meet. Elevation is relative to sincerity of aspiration and sincerity of effort at realisation.

Grace is the redeeming function of Love, wherein its expression is mellowed by the humane touch. Love redeems us by grace, and fulfils us by its elevating impulse.The movement of love is higher than the movement of grace. Love is the plant in the heavenly soil. Grace is a redeeming function of Love. Grace redeems us from earthly nature and introduces to Love. It is the intermediary between life and love.

Mystical life is essentially withdrawnness and concentration upon the finer ascents. There is the persistent demand of the evolution and expression of spirit with all its fineness and grace; and the dis-cordance that is felt in life, rightly understood, is the call for the life of higher harmony and bliss. The mystical ways are evident to those who are in deep sympathy with life and the greatest art of mystical life is to get access to the deeper currents of spirit which naturally carry, like the proverbial bird on its wings, the soul towards the light beyond all darkness, the knowledge beyond all lethe and oblivion. The sacred inspiration is often defeated by the forces hostile to progress and by the wrong ways of life. The mystic is nothing, if not an adventurer. The unconscious drift of his being is to-wards the cosmic life and cosmic sympathies and naturally he cannot forego the secret call of his nature. The seeker experiences bitter conflicts between the wonted course and the secret urge; and when the conflict is not resolved there is the visitation of grace. Grace is the uplifting force that helps when the spiritual equilibrium is lost. It sheds new light on the path when the soul struggles in darkness. Its appearance is sudden. Its ministration is unexpected. It sheds even light in the midst of mistifying darkness. It is a force, a light, a power which it is not for the seeker to command, but to follow. It helps when the animal faith is an insufficient guide and the course and expression of life offer inadequate satisfaction. Grace is the visitation and the awakening of spirit in the natural conflict of life. It lifts the veil of *Māyā* (Ignorance) and sanctions movements in consonance with spirit. It reflects spirits in the realm of nature in order that nature may take the formation of spirit. Without grace our formation, however forceful and beautiful, cannot have the dignified expression of spirit. Grace is the descending of spirit in order that the spirit in man may overcome the limitations of nature and radiate the sublimber beauties. It is expression of spirit in nature. It is the power of spirit over nature.

Grace is relative to merit. Sometimes Grace indicates God's solicitude to redeem. Love in its spiritual spontaneity is its highest ideal. The best expression of spirit is possible in unqualified and unmerited Love. Love is zealous and delicate. In entering into the forms of love and its expression a word must be said about the so-called anthropomorphic nature of these spiritual feelings and reactions. Anthropomorphic, no doubt, they are as the analogy of these expressions and reactions are drawn from our human life, but these feelings are divine in which man as man has risen much above the scale of ordinary human being. In personal life and its relations the divine Life and Truth reach their highest consummation. It does not lack in cosmic feelings, but far exceeds them in their joy and delicacy of movement, Life herein takes supra-cosmic expression. Love is divine. It is all-embracive. It works as the force of attraction, projection, growth and development in the order of evolution in nature. It works as the force of integration in family and society; it works as the force of aspiration in spirit; finally it expresses itself in divine subtlety, fineness, radiance, beauty and in power and majesty. Love is the fundamental principle emerging in various forms throughout the grades of existence.

CHAPTER-XVI

Forms of Love

Love has varied forms, colours and intensities. The Vaiṣṇavas, following human analogy, describe the forms of love and towards God. It may have a pensive expression. It is then called, śānta, dominant more in knowledge than in feeling. This is calm repose based as it is upon the sense of wideness. There is no intensive vibration in our spiritual or psychic being. Next comes the phase in which the devotes has the consciousness and the movement of being as a humble dependent and a servant of the divine. Next comes the friendship with God on intimate terms of equality. God is a lover and an associate. The sense of distance of the above two stages is minimised. The spiritual attachment becomes greater. Love manifests its still higher expression when it has taken charge of the divine as its own ward. Here in the character of love is changed and the consciousness is changed from seeking protection to giving protection to the Divine. Next to the conception of the divine child is the conception of the divine Bride-groom. This is supposed to be the highest expression of Love, as Love it is all focussed in God, without the least thought of itself. It is the divine amour. All these appear as the affiliation of human feelings to the divine, but in reality they far exceed human ways. These are the fruits of the spiritualisation of our being and in their finest expression, human ways are completely over-shadowed, though at times our human feelings are also stirred and reinforced by them. The incompatibility between the divine transfiguration and the human expression is evident, still human expression exhibits at times the divine tremor of being under the possession of spirit. The full spiritual expression is not possible unless the incompatibility is redeemed. There is a growing sense of personality as love rises in the scale.

The expression of life on its transcendental reaches is not possible unless the vital and the mental being move in tune with the graces of the spirit. The blessings of Love are to be enjoyed here, but nature raises obstructions to the privileges and possibilities. They can hardly shape themselves unless the total being is surrendered to Love. Love is the greatest transforming force, it removes all barriers from its path, not by rejecting nature, but by shaping it for its purpose. This transforming force exists in the divine potencies (the *śaktis*) which are infused into our being with new aspiration for the divine life.

Passions are spiritualised. Human impulses are divinised. The dynamism of life with all its impulses cannot be suppressed. It is to be transformed by setting up the divine consciousness. Our vital, emotional and spiritual being must be in harmony within us, if spiritual life is to be an actuality, Vaiṣṇavism establishes this harmony by making all personal relations centred in the divine. It is indeed a fine art making every movement blissful and graceful by transforming it by the impress of spirit.

Religion makes life artistic in its expression. It essentially makes the whole being a movement in harmony; and art is creative harmony. When the absorbing impulse dies, the radiant memory finds expression in artistic activity. Spirit establishes harmony in creativeness. But its greatest impulse is towards self-effacement in the loved object. It is God-intoxication. Love is spiritual liquor.

Love survives by union and separation. The separation

makes the memory of union intense and makes the understanding clear. This clear understanding of the joys of love and its sportive and artful expressions in union makes the feelings deep and intensive. Sometimes the intensity goes so deep that Love makes an idealistic creation of its own object and enjoys the ideal union with all its intensities and varieties. This ideal union reveals a phase of an identity of being of the lover and the loved. It is not present in the normal union effected by Love. The reason is the intensity of feeling. This identity is the ideal creation of this intensity. Spiritual consciousness gets a further opening not ordinarily accessible. This is really enjoying the intensities of spiritual feelings through memories. Spirit acts upon our whole being through the ideal creation of memory. This ideal projection is intensely gratifying, since it illustrates the assimilation of Love in the unconscious life process, which helps the process of transformation. But the acme of realisation is reached, when in the infinite oscillation a poise and an equilibrium are established in the intensiveness of attraction and attachment. Here the centrifugal character of Love is exhibited. It is a new experience, almost an absorption, in which the sense of individuality is for the moment overshadowed, in order that it may again reappear with higher acceleration, and with newer harmonies and deeper intensities. Love alternates between absorption and expression. In its intensive penetration there are varied expressions in the unfolding process; in the acme of realisation, the lover becomes one with the beloved. There is a lull in expression and love expresses its integral nature, where the dynamical expressions are suspended. This is a temporary phase and is followed by more peaceful and delicate movements. Love can never forsake its dynamical nature even in absorption. It is a realisation of the dynamical identity which is peculiar to love, though in it there is the apparent cessation of expression.

Love here actively seeks fusion and naturally reveals a phase which is not covered by the immediacy of relation. It is the immediacy of concentration. There is no end to the infinite variations of movement and expression, though there is occasional equilibrium in order to restore greater strength and energy. The indrawn urge of Love is followed by the display of outward energy. The more the outward expression is assimilated, the inner movement grows intensive and vigorous; and the finer orders of existence in the supra-cosmic world are revealed. Evolution in man cannot stop unless man rises quite free from nature's domination and realises in him a principle not emerging from nature—a spiritual principle which can discover in itself a direct touch and connexion with the divine. The pressing urge in evolution is really towards this fulfilment. Evolution is ultimately a rediscovery of the ultimate *good* that is realising itself through stir and strees. Nature is not blind. It is not mechanistic. It is the expression of a spiritual urge to enact a spiritual drama in creation; nature's conflicts awaken us to this consciousness. Conflicts emerge from the oblivion and forgetfulness of the spiritual urge and its play.

CHAPTER-XVII

Spiritual Ascent

The five stages of love represent in the ascending order the intensity and the richness of spiritual undulations, they draw out manifold notes of delicate vibrations and swift expressions. The intensity of interest determines the superiority of the stages, but they have not the least reference to self and all are directed to the divine. The offering of the whole being makes the finest expression of Love. Love is a delicate plant. It cannot grow in divine beauty if there is the least denial or refusal from within or even if there is the insistence for some crude satisfaction of our being. It creates a natural opposition between self and love. Love is the sacrifice of the self. It is self-offering. The self offering is complete in divine amour. With such offering distance is completely withdrawn. A new spiritual expression takes place. A dynamical identification between the Lover and the Loved is established. The divine exhibits itself is the lover as well as the beloved and love expresses itself as the divine thread of connexion between the two phases of the divine existence. God is the Lover, God is the beloved. When this conception dawns upon us, the complete spiritualisation and the divinisation of being takes place. Life in Love is really an ascent towards this realisation, for Love is this greatest spiritualising force. The Divine alone plays with the divine. This release of our divine nature is the first promise of Love. It then exhibits itself in infinite richness of life. Love cannot live without this richness. The Redemption, it gives, is not its finest privilege. The eternal movement and play which it offers are its greatest promise.

There are two kinds of dynamic identification : identification in power and identification in love. The former is necessary for cosmic purposes and may inspire souls for such events. But the finest identification is possible in Love, where life unfolds divine Love. The dynamic identification is enjoyed in its finest form through Love, for it is unfettered by earthly purpose. This dynamic identification has degrees. There may be identification in the form of occassional or continuous possession. The former fulfils some divine purpose. The latter is a rare possibility with the elect. The dynamic identification is better illustrated in the order of emanations. and hypostases, for here the divine manifests its own majesty and power in varying proportions according to the task to be fulfilled. They receive the direct influence and move in conscious identity but they have a hierarchy according to their intensity of identification and capacity of reflecting the divine power and intelligence. These emanations represent the order of perfected existence. Their perfection is determined by the intensity of the spiritual ingression. The cosmic powers are great divine agencies, but they cannot reflect the supra-cosmic expression and movements. That is a quite different order beyond the creative order, where the touch and the impress of the divine in its supra-cosmic nature is felt. Here is the divine Love exhibited, for the divine Love is really supra-cosmic, transcendent force, far beyond the cosmic forces and powers. Naturally its expressions have reference to human impulses, though at times it can filter down and give new formations to them.

This identification in power is a great opening in mystical consciousness. But the Vaiṣṇavas do not lay much emphasis on it, in as much as it still confines us to the work of cosmic powers and movements, and cannot introduce us to the finer realm of love. Yet this movement and education of consciousness should not be neglected, for it acquaints us with the Divine will and its effectiveness in creation, making at times our will identical with the Divine, and the divine movement of our being possible. Identification of will precedes identification in Love; the former is an identification necessary for the cosmic purpose, the latter is purely a personal beatification in which an order of spiritual values is revealed. Evolution of spirit proceeds this way; the finest evolution in spirit exceeds the graceful and effective movement of spirit through nature. It is naturally a sequence in mystical consciousness that follows the spirit's cosmic functioning through nature. This consciousness becomes clear, as it becomes free from the limitation of its normal functioning through the objective mind, which only reflects the relational experience but not the outspread vastness of being and its fine formations in the super-conscient reaches. The ordinary intelligence cannot realise the possibilities that lie hidden in our conscious life and its wide horizon. A section of the conscious is presented to us, while its vast range lies hidden from us.

The Vaiṣṇavas discover this by freeing consciousness from its mental restriction. Consciousness is not mentality, mentality is imposed upon it, it limits it. Consciousness freed from this limitation immediately realises its direct touch and fellowship with the divine. It is a realisation at a point in our being, where some kind of identification and nearness is directly felt. It is a realisation through total being and through life. It does not give an intellectual illumination through wise passiveness; it is a realisation through our integral being. It makes our composite being intensively dynamical. It is a mistake to suppose that Vaiṣṇavism indulges in a kind of spiritual emotionalism, leaving the other parts of out being unaffected and unillumined. The mistake becomes evident when the dynamical transformation of our total being is clearly understood. Vaiṣṇavism, in a sense, presents a completer mysticism in as much as it embraces life in its transcendental reaches and immanental expression, and the integral spirituality leaves no part of our being and its manifestation out of consideration; on the other hand it wants to envisage the full play of the divine life through all grades of existence. The opening of the higher consciousness does not exclude or reject its lower strata, but rather indicates its place in it and adds a new meaning and charm to it. As the access to higher zones of existence is attained, the limitation of our being is removed and our existence in the same zone and orbit of the divine life is felt. The natural is not completely separated from the supernatural; and the life-current flows from the super-natural into the natural, just as the natural life-current becomes more refined and gets access to the super-natural. Life is a continuous thread and in the process of evolution the thread is not cutt off, though there is the constant infiltration of the higher into the lower, and the constant access of the lower to the higher. The spiritual ascent is indicated by the enlargement of consciousness, by its infinite wideness. The perception of wideness is not here abstract, but there is a reference to a concrete centre. Cosmic pointedness is what characterises true spirituality. Though Vaiṣṇavism favours the eternal flow and infinite undulation of spirit, it does not favour the idea of spiritual life as cosmic pointlessness; spiritual life rises in vaster expansion, but always with reference to a centre of existence. It is not eccentric. It is in the terminology of Vaiṣṇavism, strictly to belong to the orbit of the divine existence, called *Sālokya Mukti*. The word 'Mukti' is here important, it is a liberation from the restricted movement of being and consciousness and entering into a supra-mental vastness. It is the first access to the divine order. It is really unfolding in consciousness, when a finer and holier and a vaster expression becomes quite evident to us. Next follows the consciousness of union with the divine. Consciousness gets into supreme touch with the divine and feels the impress of a relation with it. Life moves now with its focus in the divine. Though everything moves within the orbit of divine consciousness, still everything may not enjoy its direct touch and its influence. *Sājujya Mukti* gives this blessed privilege. In dynamic spirituality the fellowship does not imply assimilation. It implies imbibing an influence. The next stage is *Svārupya. Svārupya* endows us with the divine nature and engrafts upon us divine possibility. In the ascent of life, such a consciousness emerge and it strikes the beginning of the dynamic identification. The dynamic identification is exhibited at its finest when the divine power is installed in us, when we acquire the power of hastening evolution by influencing the creative potencies. Spiritual evolution implies, along with the widening of consciousness, a kind of oneness with the divine force that is functioning in the different planes of existence. This assimilation is not an abstract possibility, but a concrete fact which becomes self-evident with the psychic and the spiritual opening in our being. One reads of Yogic powers and possibilities that emerge on the path. these powers generally coincide with dematerialisation and psychic transference which indicate conquest of nature, but finer powers emerge when the dynamic identification is well-laid in our being and this identification gives complete control over nature, and the divine will becomes actively manifest through our being. The divine will sometimes selects fit instruments for a divine purpose and possesses them—but that is an occasional event in the regulation of the universe, and it is essentially a matter of divine descent and divine interference. But the dynamic identification is essentially and ascent and a deeper penetration into being where our natural limitations are removed and consciousness enjoys a direct inspiration and identification with the divine. It is a movement of spirit in spirit itself. It is an expression far beyond cosmic life. It is not fettered by cosmic activities. Power is not the best exhibition of the divine. Power is displaced by love and grace. Love is a freer movement than Power and even Grace. It is the divine life in excelsis. Hegel speaks of the Absolute Life as the eternal play of love with itself. It has neither finality nor purpose. It is the highest rhythm of life, swiftest in movement, most delicate in expression and absorbing in harmony. It is the highest fecundity of life. It is the divine passion which attracts but does not bind. It is the divine impulse which absorbs but is not lost.

Love reacts upon every plane of existence from the crudest to the finest; it has expression in inconscient matter, in vital life, in vital emotions, in psychic attractions but these are not its finest expressions. Here its expression is interfered with because of the medium and naturally its grace is released in supra-mental planes, where it is realised in its infinite elasticity and transparent beauty.

CHAPTER-XVIII

Emotional Ecstasy

Vaiṣṇavism has a natural influence and attraction because of the emotional stir it produces—and the emotional satisfaction it enhances. Even competent thinkers have erroneously identified religion with emotional enthusiasm (*e.g.*, Whitehead). Rupa and Sanātana Goswāmī emphasise the emotional colouring in spirituality. And the exhibition of emotional outbursts in spiritual ecstacy lends weight to the usual opinion.

The excessive stress upon Love in Vaiṣṇavism should not make Vaiṣṇavism pass for emotionalism. It is a common mistake that is made. There is an essential difference between emotionalism and spirituality. Emotionalism is associated with our mental and vital being, spirituality is not, though it can influence them both. Love is the finest expression of the spirit, and the spirit is different from mind or even intelligence. Spiritual expressions are vibrative but calm. They do not in the least perturb the inner peace, or tranquility, however intense be the consciousness. It disturbs the equilibrium of the psychic and the vital being only because they are not sufficiently transformed to bear the intensive spiritual out-pouring and expression. The discharge of the intense psychic energy which goes with spiritual intuitions or perception cannot be received by the mental of vital being without a reaction, because they are not accustomed to high pressure. Naturally obstruction is set up in the mind or vital being and confusion follows. When there is not the least resistance to the spiritual discharge either from the vital or the mental body, there are no perturbations. Spirit is intensely active and impressive and evokes *response*. What will be the kind of reaction depends upon the character of the constitution. Devotional mysticism feels the touch of the spirit primarily in the heart centre and naturally it generates various *shades* in *feelings*. But if the devotee is not overcome therewith, he can follow it in knowledge and action. Spirituality affects all the parts of our being and can quicken all the fibres of our constitution to an intensive degree. Its character depends upon the part of our being affected by its ingress. It stirs the will, stimulates the heart and quickens the intellect. The spirit can affect our psychic and vital being. It can fulfil all the demands of our being. The finest phase of love can be revealed in benign serenity and sovereign calm. Even love presupposes this unruffled calm. The finest spiritual force is released in calm. Love quickens up life response. But this does not imply that there must be oscillations upsetting serenity with which spirituality is essentially connected. If there is distance it indicates that in our constitution there is some part which cannot bear the pressure. In mystical life our psychological constitution is worked up to a great intensity and as, Alexis Carrel has said, it brings into play some parts of our nervous being which ordinarily in man do not function. Nature wonderfully helps and gradually under the pressure makes the system ready for the reflection of a higher spiritual charge. Obstruction may be overcome with judicious guidance. The finest harmony is established in all parts of our being and all react harmoniously to the spiritual current and spiritual aspiration. In the life of the ardent mystic the central motive becomes so dominant that all other motives are lost in it, or become contributory to it. So long as the lower vital urges are insistent it is difficult to get the full result. Still the spiritual urges cannot be missed. The inner conflict must disappear before the full result can be obtained. Before the pilgrim's progress is completed, the seeker will have to pass through "the sloughs of despond." It is natural. Mysticism is a new life, a new birth into immeasurable possibilities. The birth pangs are to be borne patiently and calmly before the finest emergence is possible.

Chapter-XIX

TANTRA
Occultism and Spirituality

Meditation

In order to realize *Īśvara-tattva* (God-consciousness), the *Sādhaka* has to proceed in the path of meditation which will lead him to the graduated participation in the consciousness of this enveloping fullness of divinity. The divine consciousness manifests itself in stages in the evolutionary processes of the universe when each being or each object becomes a part of that consciousness. These all-pervading consciousness splits itself into individual bodies and objects by assuming different physical forms. This consciousness is indivisible, indestructible and immortal.

Meditation is not a psychological act or a physical movement, but a trans-empirical attitude. The philosophical foundations and the religious consequences of self-analysis in meditation accelerates the ascent of the self to the higher level. When the understanding expands itself to the dimension of a universal presence, it reaches the complex or enclosure of meditation, and the phenomenal intellect beocmes naturally conditioned by space, time and cause. While in meditation, one enters into a state of conscious aloneness which is in harmony with the reality of nature. Deep meditation is a state of conscious death or sleep and rather a conscious dissociation of oneself from all relationship with the external world.

In meditation, a *Sādhaka* has to pass through three preliminary stages : *śravaṇa*, *manana*, and *nididhyāsana*. After listening or studying under a preceptor, the aspirant can know the path of knowledge. It is called *śravaṇa* (hearing). Then a personal in-depth analysis grows in his mind about the lessons. This stage is called *manana* (thinking). The truth that is communicated to him is now absorbed into his mind. This self-absorption is called *nididhyāsana*, the sinking of these truths from the conscious level into the deeper levels of self. In *nididhyāsana*, the unconsciousness is roused into activity, and the whole one's being is meditating.

Śravaṇa, manana and *nididhyāsana* are the traditiona' practices in meditation. In this stage of meditation, the unconsciousness is roused into activity and the whole of one's being becomes enlightened when the *chit* (consciousness) gradually melts into *sat* (truth), and the result that is achieved is *ananda* (bliss).

Śakti

What is covered by *śakti* is the principle of *Para-brahman* called Śiva.

There are three kinds of *śakti* : one is *Janma-siddha śakti* with which one is born and which continues to the end of the life. The second is the *Mādhyamika śakti* that manifests and takes root when the mind is developed and its faculties or the faculties of the heart get ripen. It springs to birth in what is called the *bodha-avasthā*. The third is the *Kṣaṇika śakti* that is active in movements when one is engaged in favourable activities like *pūja, dhyāna, japa*, holy company etc., when things propitious for the breath of the higher power. Usually, this *śakti* stays as long as one lives in that atmosphere and withdraws when one comes out of it. But it one cultivates is properly, then the *Kṣaṇika śakti* develops into *Mādhyamika śakti* and may even manifest as the *Janma-siddha śakti* in the next birth.

The Śaivism system upholds the existence of three ultimate principles : (i) Śiva, the supreme all-doing, all-knowing, all-sustaining Being called *Prakāśa*; (ii) *Śakti*, a personal entity of the nature of Perfect Egoity; and (iii) *Aṇu*, the individual soul under the bondage of impurities of limitations. Of these three, the greater prominence is attributed to the idea of *śakti*. In Śiva, remains His *śakti* or Nature in a sort of reflex relation of Self-Identity. Then as He comes to possess the tendency of projecting Himself this *śakti* evolves from Him in the form of Divine Creative Will (*Icchatvam*).

Thus *śakti* is that power of freely willing Nature of Śiva which is related to him in Self-identity, and the conception of *śakti* as Śiva's nature of perfect freedom is further defined as the vibration of consciousness of real Egoity holding within itself and visualizing the entire world or objects as 'this is'. To make it clear, it can be said that *śakti* is the unalienated conscious nature of Śiva with all its contents unmanifested. *Śakti* can never be conceived as a mere abstract principle devoid of all concrete contents. She is the power or capability of knowing and acting of the self-established Śiva. *Śakti* is the Divine Nature which supplies the ground of Śiva's realization of His own self.

Puruṣa and Prākṛti

Eternal Śiva is known as *Nirguṇa* and *Saguṇa*. *Nirguṇa* is dissociated from *Prākṛti* and *Saguṇa* is associated with *Prākṛti*. Thus it can be seen that in the beginning there were two ultimate principles : Śiva and *Prākṛti*, the principle of consciousness and the principle of unconsciousness. It may look like Sāṁkhya dualism, but it is not so. Because in Sāṁkhya, the unconcious *Prākṛti* is the cause, and there is no room for God or *Īśvara*. Nor it is dualism of the Yoga system of Patañjali, for therein an individual, enjoying freedom from the troubles of the world, is the *Īśvara*, and *Prākṛti* is the cause. But the supreme *Īśvara* who is rich in the wealth of *Sat-Chit-Ananda* (Existence-Consciousness-Bliss) and associated with *Prakriti*, is the cause.

Pañcha Bhūta

Pañcha Bhūta or the five *bhūtas* (existents) are forms of *śakti* (energy). The energy in *ākāśa* (space) is called *Śāntyatita*,the very quiescent. The energy in *vāyu* (vital air) is *Śānti*, the quiescent. That in *tejas* (hear and light) is *Vidyā*, the Enlightener. That in *apa* (the fluids) is *Pratiṣṭha*, the Stay. And in the *kṣiti* (earth) is called *Nivṛtti*, the Final. All these form *nāda*, the conscious energy in vibration which is personified in Brahma, the creator or *kriyā-śakti* (action-energy) who is the resultant of the coalescence of *Rudra*, the *Ichchhā-śakti* (volition-energy), and *Viṣṇu*, the *Jñāna-śakti* (Cognition energy).

Among the five *bhūtas*, ether is transparent, Air is black, Fire red, Water white, and Earth yellow. The region of Ether is circular, that of Air is hexagonal, of Fire is triangular, of Water is of the form of a half-moon with a lotus therein, and that of that Earth is square in shape. The regions or *maṇḍalas* of the five *bhūtas* contain the letters which belong to the *different bhūtas*. The letters are classified into five categories according to the number of the *bhūtas*. The five *bhūtas* again originate from the five *kalās* : *Nivṛtti*, *Pratiṣṭhā*, *Vidyā*, *Śānti* and *Śāntyatita* which in their turn have originated from *Nāda*.

The Supreme Lord

The Supreme Lord in the only efficient cause, *Prakṛti*, His Divine Nature, who is inseparable from Him, is the formal cause, and *Bindu* or Matter is the material cause of this universe. These three ultimate factors and their relation with one another have been clearly defined with a special reference to actual visualisaion and ultimate realisation ending in *tattvajñāna* (the knowledge of the True Self) which alone leads to *mokṣa* (liberation). The cause of this world is viewed under three heads : *Nimitta Kāraṇa* (efficient cause), *Upādāna Kāraṇa* (material cause) and *Sahakāri Kāraṇa* (formal cause).

The Supreme Lord's inherent powers of *dṛk* (Supreme consciousness) and *kriyā* (action) are the two correlated aspects of His eternal transcendent power. Everthing in this universe emanates from Him. He is the Lord over all, while He himself knows no Lord. He is in every object of this phenomenal world as the One Supreme and Omnipresent essential spirit, while He Himself is above *Māyā* in all circumstances. He is infinite who always transcends the universe. It is through the grace of His *Anugraha Śakti* that the devotees attain salvation.

The Supreme Self (Śiva) acts as Śakti of the Universe. His efficiency is manifested through His five Divine functions : *Janma* (Creation), *Sthiti* (Sustenance), *Dhvaṅgsa* (Dissolution), *Tirodhana* (Playful Obscuration) and *Anugraha* (Gracious Revelation)

Janma

The direct creations of Śiva are all transcendental in nature and are meant for rendering necessary help and guidance to the beings created through His *Maya śakti*. They include *Vidyā*, *Vidyeśvaras* and others who are all pure and dinvine, having their origin from the All-pure, the Supreme Śiva, the Absolute. They are also termed 'Śiva' and 'Śakti' accordingly as they are masculine or feminine. All manifestations from Śiva are called *janma* (creation).

Sthiti

Sthiti (Sustenance) means that function of the Almighty due to which the universe maintains an orderly method of existence, growth and development, and the created beings exist to serve their respective purposes according to the Divine dispensation.

Dhvaṅgsa

Dhvaṅgsa (Dissolution) is principally divided into three kinds : *Adhama* (Lowest), *Madhyama* (Medium) and *Uttama* (Highest).

The form of dissolution, which takes place at the time of nocturnal repose of the Brahma (the God of Creation) when the first three *lokas* (regions) of the universe viz., *Bhuloka*, *Bhubarloka* and *Svarloka* are dissolved, is called *Adhama Laya* (*Dhvaṅgsa*).

When at night, Śrikaṇṭha (another God representing a different aspect of the creative energy) is at rest, all the *tattvas* (principles) beginning from *Pṛthvī Tattva* and ending in *Guṇa Tattva* ard dissolved. This process is termed *Madhyama Laya*.

At the time of *Mahapralaya* (final dissolution), everything, visible or invisible, with the exception of *Māyā Puruṣa* and Śiva are dissolved. The dissolution is called *Uttama Pralaya*.

Śiva, the Supreme Lord, is the efficient cause of all these forms of *Pralaya* (*dhvaṅgsa*).

Tirodhana

Tirodhana (Playful obscuration) is the peculiar indescribable functions, throgh which the Omnipresent Almighty veils Himself from the individualised and embodied self.

Anugraha

Anugraha or *Vimukti* (Gracious Revelation) means the function, through which the *jīvas* or *paśus* are liberated from the bonds of illusion and matter. The revelations which are by nature pure and true lead to the Ultimate Truth.

The All-Merciful Lord Śiva who is the only granter of liberation, reveals His true nature only to competent devotees and thus grant them the *Kaivalya* or *Mukti* (absoluteness or liberation). This vindicates usefulness of worship which leads to the knowledge of the Supreme Being

Kuṇḍalinī

The *Kuṇḍalinī Yoga* is very much practised by the advanced *Tāntrikas* who are called *Kaulas*, well-acquainted with the passage of *Kuṇḍalinī (Kula-patha)* through the three *liṅgas* which represent the three aspects of *sthūla* (gross) *sūkṣma* (subtle) and *kāraṇa* (causal) and attain the *turiya* (fourth) stage which is beyond them (*bhavatita*) and is the excellent abode of the *Guru* or the *Parama Śiva*. This state is to be achieved by passing through the three subordinate *bhāvas* : *paśu bhāva* (in bonds of animal propensities), *vīra-bhāva* (the stage when the *Sādhaka* is ready to face and struggle to cut the bonds of *māyā*), and the *divya-bhāva* (the stage in which the divination of the individual self sets in, and there is an end to all forms of dualism). These *bhāvas* are attainable by passing through seven different *acharas* or stages of purification and modes of *sādhanā* which have correspondence and correlation with the seven principal *chakras* (centres) in the subtle body, and the seven planes of knowledge of Vedānta philosophy.

The *Mūlādhāra Chakra* or the lotus located below the genitals and above the anus has four petals with *va, ca, sha,* and *sa* letters. In the pericarp of this lotus is the square of *dharā* (earth) of yellow and a beautiful *maṇḍala* with eight spears around it, and within it is *Pṛthvī Bīja Lam* which has four arms and is seated on the *airāvata*. Inside the *bindu* of the above *bīja* is seated the infant *Brahma* who has four faces and four hands holding the staff, goad, rosary and the gesture of *abhaya* which dispels fear. The *Devī Ḍākini*, red in colour with four hands holding *śūla* (spear), *khatvāṅga* (staff), *khaḍga* (sword) and *chaṣaka* (drinking cup), is seated on the lotus. *Kandarpa vāyu* and *kāma vāyu*, both of which are red, are also within the lightning-like triangle called *traipura*. Above this, is *śyāmavarṇa* (colour of green leaf) *Sayambhu Linga*, and above and around this, is *Kuṇḍalinī* coiled three and half times in Her shining snake-like form. It is She who maintains all the beings of the world and shines in the cavity of the root (*mūla*) lotus, like a chain of brilliant lights.

Svādhiṣṭhāna Chakra is the vermillion coloured lotus placed at the root of the genitals. It has six petals of the colour of lightning with six letters *ba, bha, ma, ya ra*, la with *bindus* over them. In the pericarp of this lotus is the white region of water with a half-moon in its centre. The *Varuṇa Bīja Vaṁ* is seated inside it on the *makara* with a noose in its hands. Within the *bindu* is *Viṣṇu* seated on *Garuḍa*. He has four hands holding *śaṅkha* (conch-shell), *chakra* (discus), *gadā* (mace) and *padma* (lotus). He is dressed in yellow raiment and wears a garland of wild flowers round his neck and is youthful in appearance with the mark of *śrivatsa* and the gem *kaustubha* on his chest. In the pericarp is also *śyāma-varṇa Śakti Rākini* with four hands, holding *śūla* (spear), *abja* (lotus), *ḍarmaru* (drum) and *ṭaṅka* (battle-axe). She is three-eyed with projecting and terrible teeth, found of while rice, with a stream of blood flowing through a nostril.

In *Maṇipūra Chakra,* the lotus at the level of the navel bears the colour of a heavy rain-cloud. It has ten petals with ten letters of lustrous blue colour : *da, dha, na, ta, tha, da, dha, na, pa, pha* with *bindus* above each of them. In the pericarp of this lotus is the region of fire which is red and triangular in shape, and outside it, on its three sides are three *svattika* marks, and within the triangle is the *bīja* or fire *Ram,* red in colour, seated on a ram with four arms holding *vajra* (thunderbolt), *śakti* (rapier), and gestures of the *vara* and *abhaya*. In the *bindu* of *Vahni Bīja*, *Rudra* of red colour, old in appearance, is seated on a bull. His skin appears to be while being besmeated with ashes. On a red lotus, in the pericarp of this lotus, is seated the blue *Lākini Śakti* with three faces having three eyes in each. She is four-armed with *vajra* (thunderbolt), *śakti* (rapier), and signs of *vara* and *abhaya*. She has fierce projecting teeth and is fond of rice cooked with *dāl* (pulse) and fresh meat full of blood, and she is exhilarated with divine wine (*varuṇi*) dedicated by here devotees.

Anāhata Chakra (heart lotus) is red (of the colour of *bandhuka* flower), having twelve petals with twelve letters of vermillion colour *ka, kha, ga, gha, nga, cha, chha, ja, jha, na, ta, tha*, with *bindus* over them. In its pericarp is the hexagonal smoke-coloured *vāyu-maṇḍala* (region of air), and above it, *sūrya-maṇḍala* (region of sun) with a triangle, lustrous as ten million flashes of lightning within it. *Bīja* of air (*vāyu*) *yam* of a smoky hue, seated on a *kṛṣṇasāra* (antelope) with four arms and carrying the weapon *ankusa* (goad). The three-eyed Īśa *(Īśvara)* of the colour of a swan and with two hands bearing the gestures *vara* and *abhaya* is within the *bindu* of the *bīja*. In the pericarp of this lotus is the golden-hued *Kākini Śakti* with four arms carrying *pāśa* (noose), *kapāla* (skull), and signs of *vara* and *abhaya* with her heart softened with nectar, dressed in yellow garment and various jewelleries along with a garland of dried bones. In the centre of the *trikoṇa* is *Śiva* in golden *Banaliṅga* form, like shining gold with c̄reated moon and *bindu* on his head. He looks resplendant with a rush of desire. Below his is *jīvātman* (embodied self) like *haṁ-saḥ* as the steady flame of a lamp in a windless place. Below the pericarp of this lotus is an eight-petalled red lotus with its head turned upwards, which is meditated as the seat of the Deity in mental worship. In it, there are the *kalpavṛkṣa* (celestial wish-granting tree): *Maṇipītha* (the jewelled alter) decorated wtih flags, canopy etc.

Viṣuddhi Chakra (lotus of purification) is situated at the base of the throat with sixteen petals of smoky purple colour with all the sixteen vowels of crimson hue, having the *bindus* above them. In its paricarp is the *nabho maṇḍala* (eternal region), circular in shape and white like the full moon. Inside it is the *chandra maṇḍala* (the lunar region), and above it is the white *Vyoma Bīja Haṁ* seated on a snow-white elephant and endowed with four hands holding *pāśa, aṅkuśa* and making gestures of *vara* and *abhaya*. Within the *bindu* is *Ardhanārīśvara Sadā Śiva* with three eyes, five faces and ten beautiful arms and clothed in tiger-skin. His body is united with that of *Girijā* and is seated on a great lion seat placed on the back of a bull. He is of golden colour in the left and snow-white in the right. In his hands he holds the *śūla* (trident), the *ṭaṅka* (battle-axe), the *khaḍga* (sacrificial sword), the *vajra* (thunderbolt), *dahana* (fire arms), the *Nāgendra* (the king of snakes), the *ghaṇṭa* (bell), the *aṅkuśa* (goad), the *pāśa* (noose) and mark of the *abhaya* (fear-dispelling) *mudrā* (posture) and his whole body is smeared with ashes, and his neck is adorned with a garland of snakes. He is seen like a mountain which is both silvery and golden. The down-turned digit (*kāla*) of the moon which constantly drops nectar is on his forehead. Within the pericarp and in the lunar region is the *Śakti Śākini*, white in colour, four-armed, three-eyed, having five faces clothed in yellow, carrying in her hands a bow and an arrow, a noose and a goad. She is the *Devatā* of *asthi* (bone), *dhātu* and maddens all the mass of the *paśus*.

Ajñā Chakra (the two-petalled lotus which when reached reveals the *ajñā* or the commands of the great *Guru* seated on the *Sahasrāra Padma*) is situated between the eyebrows. On its two petals are the letters *ha, kṣa* which are also white and enhance its beauty. The *Hākini Śakti* having six faces with three eyes in each, is seated on the pericarp, Her six arms hold *vara* and *abhaya mudrās*, rosary, human skull, a small drum and a book. Above her within a *trikoṇa* (triangle) is *Itara-Liṅga* shining like a chain of lightning flashes. The first *bīja* of Vedas (*praṇava*) is also here. Above this, within another *trikoṇa* is *Antarātman* (Inner self) resembling a flame in its radiance. On its four sides are sparks, surrounding a light which by its own lustre makes visible and distinct all that exists between *mūla* and *Brahmarandhra*. Above this again is *manas,* and above *Manas chakra* is the *Soma chakra* (the region of full moon). Within this is the *Bīja Haṁsaḥ*. In its lap is the Omnipotent *Paraśiva* with *Siddha-Kāli* in the left, the very Self of Eternal Bliss.

Sahasrāra (Thousand-petalled Lotus) *Chakra* : Above *Ajñā Chakra* is the form of *mahānāda,* the place where *vāyu* cease to be and the pure intelligence (*buddhi)* becomes manifest. Above all these, is the *parama vyoma* (the supreme ether) wherein is Śāṅkhini nādi and below the visarga is the white thousand-petalled lotus with the petals turned downwards and its clustered filaments tinged with the colour of the rising sun. The fifty letters of the alphabet 'a' to 'ia' which are also whitish in colour, go round and round its petals twenty times. Within the lotus is the full moon shedding profuse rays, moist and cool like nectar. Inside it constantly shining like lightning, is the *Akathadi* triangle and inside this again shines *mahaśūnya* (the great void) which is the excellent *bindu* attainable by great effort only and is worshipped in secret by Devas and *Kaula Sādhakas*. It is the chief centre of liberation manifesting the pure *Nirvāṇa Kāla*, subtle like a thousandth part of a hair with the *amakāla*, the sixteenth *kāla* (digit) of the moon which is of red colour and shining like lightning. On the pericarp of this lotus is *Parama Haṁsaḥ,* and above it, on an ever-blissful and white twelve-petalled lotus is seated the *Guru* who is *Parama Śiva* himself. He is the *Paramātman* and *Brahma*.

Kuṇḍalinī is a great spiritual power hidden in male human body. Because of its coiled nature, it is called 'kuṇḍalinī'. *Kuṇḍalinī*, is supposed to be stored up at the end of the spinal cord. It is the reserve force which is psychic and spiritual. It has its effect upon the vital force and also on our physical being. It is effective only in man. It is a cosmic principle, the primal force or *Śakti* involved in all existence. So it is everywhere. It is the immanent force or will to help higher ascents in evolution. It gives spiritual foundation.

Kuṇḍalinī is the force of diffusion and expansion. The higher it goes up in its ascent through the psychic centres, the more it acquaints us with all the layers of consciousness. Finally, it touches the universal focal point and invests us with the peace that passes undestanding.

The Tantras ultimately reduce matter into a set of vibrations. Advance in spirituality is indicated by the cadence and the rhythm of sound vibrations by the aura of soft light and by bright but subdued colours. The whole being takes a delicate and attractive form. The vibrations of the psychic being, and the sound, light and colour that are experienced with the ascent of *kuṇḍalinī* are high in potency and intensive in movement.

Kulāchāra

The *Kulachuḍāmaṇi Tantra* or 'crest jewel' of the *kulachakra* division of the Tantra Cult is considered to be an authentic scripture by the worshippers of *Śakti*. It is found to be frequently referred to as an authority in many Tantric works such as *Vamakeśvara Tantra*, *Bhairavi Tantra* etc. The *Kulachuḍāmaṇi* is in the form of a dialogue in its composition—the *śāstra* being revealed by the Devi in Her form as *Bhairavi* in reply to the questions put to Her by Śiva in His form as *Bhairava*.The test is better known as *Nigama*, as opposed to *Āgama*, in which the *śāstra* is revealed by Śiva Himself, and such revelation of Śiva or Śakti is mere *līlā* (sports), since Śiva and Śakti are one and the same and it is Śiva who reveals. Śiva is, however, the revealer of the *śāstra* in all cases, figuring Himself as *Śiṣya* (disciple) or as *Guru* (teacher). In fact, the Tantra was originally revealed by Maheśvara (Śiva) who himelf stood for that purpose in the position of the *Guru* as well as that of the *Śiṣya*.

Kulāchāra is called a secret doctrine and practice. The *Bhairavi*, as discoursing of it in the *Kulachuḍāmaṇi*, says at the outset that it had not been told to Viṣṇu nor to Brahma nor to Ganapa.

Kulachuḍāmaṇi Tantra contains the innumerable names of the *Kula-sundarīs* of *Devīs* who are said to be Tripura, Kālikā, Vāgiśvari, Sukuta, Kula, Mātaṅgini, Pūrṇā, Vimalā, Chaṇḍanāyikā, Ekajaṭā, Durgā and others. A complete list of sixty-four Tantras are given in the *Vamakeśvara*.

They are: (1) Mahāmaya, (2) Śāmbara, (3) Yoginijālaśāmbara, (4) Tattva-śāmbara; and under the group of Bhairvāṣṭaka (eight Tantras): (5) Saṅghāra, (6) Āsitaṅga, (7) Rudra, (8) Chaṇḍa, (9) Krodha, (10) Unmatta, (11) Kapil, and (12) Bhiṣaṇa; and under Bahurūpāṣṭaka group the eight Tantras of the seven Mātrikās and Śivadūtis (13 to 20); and under the group of Yamalāṣṭaka the eight namely, (21) Brahmayāmala, (22) Viṣṇuyāmala, (23) Rudrayāmala, (24) Lakṣmīyāmala (25) Umāyāmala (26) Skandayāmala, (27)

Ganeśayāmala, and (28) Grahayāmala, (29) Mahochchuśya (30) Vatula, (31) Vatulottara, (32) Hṛdbheda, (33) Tantrabheda, (34) Guhyatantra, (35) Kāmika, (36) Kalāvada, (37) Kalāsāra, (38) Kubjikamata, (39) Tantrottara, (40) Vinatantra, (41) Trodala, (42) Trodalottara, (43) Pañchamrita (44) Rupabheda, (45) Bhutoddamara, (46) Kulāsāra, (47) Kuloddisha, (48) Kulachuḍāmaṇi, (49) Sarvajñānottara, (50) Mahākālimātā, (51) Mahā-Lakṣmīmātā, (52) Siddha-yogeśvarimātā, (53) Kurupikāmātā, (54) Devarūpikāmātā, (55) Sarvavīramātā, (56) Vimalāmātā, (57) (a) Purvamnaya, (b) Paścimamnaya, (c) Dakṣiṇamnaya, (d) Uttaramnaya, (58) Niruttara. (59) Vaiśeṣika, (60) Jñānarnava, (61) Virabali, (62) Aruṇeśa, (63) Mohiniśa, and (64) Viśuddheśvara.

Her Personification

The Goddess *Tripurasundari resides* in the subtle region (*chakra*) which is essentially a *bindu*, sitting in the lap of Śiva, the Lord of Love, a phase of the moon set as an ornament on Her forehead. In Her hands, She holds the noose (an emblem of the power of attachment which separates the petty self from the supreme), the goad (an emblem of the urge towards liberating knowledge), and sugarcane bow and five flowery arrows (emblematic, in the same way as 'cupid's bow' of the passion which drives a person to dedicate his senses to adoration of the *devata*).

Padukapañcakam

Padukapañcakam is the five-fold foot-stool or seat of the *Guru* (the Supreme Self) uttered from the mouth of Śiva Himself who is the revealer of all the Tantras (True knowledge). The highest form of *Tāntrika Yoga* can only be achieved by very powerful Yogīs. The supreme inherent power in the human body, which normally remains coiled or dormant like a serpent at the base of the spine, is called the *Kuṇḍalinī Śakti*. It is uncoiled and made pass through the six principal *chakras* or centres of the subtle body which are in the form of lotuses. This process generates a wonderful powers and a new vitality in the whole psychophysical organism. As it also purifies the elements of the body, it is known as *Bhūta-śuddhi*.

Mysticism

The Tantric mysticism indicates different phases in response to the definite modulations. Occultism has different shades. The spiritual tremor is felt through one's vital mental and higher mental being. It rejuvenates them and produces pleasing vibrations, but the vibrations that emanate from the depath and the height of one's being have greater value, because they touch the higher spring of life. By evoking the cosmic creative will, the Tantras displace the determination of nature and establish the indetermination of spirit. This consumma-tion becomes possible, because the Tantras realise in the *Mahāśakti* (transcendent will), the power to eventually dispense with the supposed antagonism of matter and spirit and to spiritualise matter. Matter is more a convention than acceptance. It has no reality. It originates out of the creative will in the process of emergence. The creative will has in it potency to reshape mind and matter for more exalted expression.

Science, Art and Philosophy

Mysticism reflects the whole of life, and is thus considered as the science, art and philosophy in the Tantras. As science, it advances the fine psychology of one's make-up probing deeper into its formations unearthing the forces that array themselves in the different strata of existence from the physical to the spiritual. The knowledge of forces and their interconnection and inter-dependence are necessary to set and establish definite tunes in one's being and to give them a spiritual tone.

The mysticism that is represented in the Tantras has to its advantage the wide knowledge of astral energies which silently give shape to one's psychic and vital being. Such astral forces are in direct contact with the higher forces of intelligence and spirit.

The Tantras give an occult art and estoric philosophy with a perfect vision of the forces operating in creation. The superb beauty of the Tantric wisdom lies in acquainting us with the spiritual architecture of the universe, the immanent radiant forces and the divine force in the heart of existence. Transcendence and creativeness are blended in the life of spirit and the Tantras take cognizance of both.

Consciousness

The psychological distinction of the conscious and the unconscious is anticipated in the Tantras, and in some respects their analysis is finer, their localization is more accurate. The psycho-analyst finds the libido or *elan vital* as the supreme principle and considers all finer development as ramifications of it. The unconscious may be fundamental structure not disturbed by the fluctuations of a transitory consciousness, but its nature and range still remain a mystery.

Religious Consciousness

Religion and philosophy go together in the Tantras. The religious aspiration is the yearing after the spiritual life which has two movements : to free itself from the cobweb of the mazes of life, instinctive, vital and mental, and also to establish a direct link between our central being and its existence. Religious consciousness implies the sense of the infinite, the temporary, dropping of the creative expressions and the self-surrender in the eternal silence and peace.

Trika

In Kashmir Śaivism a spiritual philosophy known as *Trika-sasana* or *Trika-śāstra* or simply 'Trika' is so called, either because it accepts as mosst important the triad—*Siddha*, *Namaka*, and *Mālinī*—out of the ninety-two *Āgamas* recognized by it; or because the triad consisting of Śiva, Śakti and Anu or Nara, or of the goddesses *Para*, *Apara*, and *Paratpara* is recognized, or because it explains three modes of knowledge of Reality viz, *abheda* (non-dual), *bheda-veda* (non-dual and dual) and *bheda* (dual). The system has two main branches : *Spanda* and *Pratyabhijña*. The *Pratyabhijña Śāstra* is really the philosophical branch of Trika.

In Trika, Reality is conceived both as transcendent and immanent. As transcendent, it is described as Śiva, which is immanent Śakti. Śiva and Śakti are two inseparable realities. They are two phases or aspects of the same Reality. Considered as purely transcendent, Śiva is *śava* (dead as it were), but in truth, there is perfect equilibrium (*samarasya)* between Śiva and Śakti, and as such the integrality is designated as *Paramaśiva*. Śakti is described as the *hṛdaya* (heart), the *sara* (essence) of Śiva. Śiva as Śakti manifests Himself as a correlated order of knowers, knowables and means of knowledge.

The Trika system conceives Śiva as *nirvikalpa*, free from *vikalpa* or determination. As Paramaśiva is the perfect inalienable identity, there is nothing from which it can be distinguished. Hence there is no *vikalpa* in Paramaśiva who is *nirvikalpa*. In the *sambhava-upāya*, the *nirvikalpa* knowledge is awakened through *dīkṣa* and all *vikalpas* are destroyed.

Occultism

Spirituality and occultism discover the immanent spirit through our nature. Then the latent forces of our nature make their appearance and show their strength and power. The Tantras speak of varied powers which are far beyond the conception of the scientific intellect, for they follow the functioning of the subtlest forces; veils after veils are withdrawn and wonderous forces under the control of the released spirit are revealed endowing it with a form of superhuman omniscience. With the functioning of *Kuṇḍalinī*, the obstruction of inner matter is withdraw from our sense, the heart, the intellect and superior organs.

There is no magic in occult science, excepting that it tunes up our being to a high pitch to acrivate our consciousness fully. In fact, occultism reaffirms our consciousness throughout our being which release the fine forces of nature and converts it gradually into a fit vehicle of the spirit. The physical, the vital and the mental—all react harmoniously to the spiritual expression and a deeper harmony is established in them. The occultist enjoys the divine harmony everywhere—inside him as well as outside of him. This harmony follows the grades of consciousness. The higher the reach, the deeper is the harmony and the greater the range of being. This is a great art of removing the contradictions of nature and establishing the identical tune everywhere. The occultists can work in all grades of consciousness and is aware of their inner-connexion.

Occultism is not to be condemned, for it is really a science, the service of which can make human life blessed than what it is generally known to us, not by magic, buit by hastening the evolution of the spirit in wisdom and power.

Occultism is the natural consequence of truly spiritual life. Mankind, in its slavery to the habits of life, is not prepared to forego them and to receive the privileges and the changes that an occult life introduces.

Occultism renders a threefold service : (1) it unearths

our hidden being; (2) it reveals a correspondence between the psychic and the cosmic forces; and (3) it discovers our central being which regulates the forces in such a way as the slavery to nature may be shaken off, and the divine will and the power be activated in us. It is associated with spirituality, which is the indrawn urge to be associated with the divine, and occultism is the natural consequence, sought or unsought. It has spontaneous expression with the spiritual aspiration.

Occultism makes the whole nature divinely activating all the parts of our being. Divine wisdom, divine movement, and divine being go together. Philosophy gives glimpses into divine wisdom. Occultism gives a new birth to our being in dynamic spirituality. It introduces a superior tone in every part of being and gradually makes it fully divine. It indicates a new line of superior spiritual evolution and seeks to change the being in its appearance by drawing out the deeper force and by activating. Occultism has its intimate relation to art and religion. It releases the creative instinct to its full height. It gives the creative exaltation, and the stream of creation flows spontaneously.

Occultism is a refined and delicate art of modulating our being with a graceful expression. The supra-conscious throws its light and influence on the sub-conscious and reveals the functioning. It establishes a harmony in the conscious life. Nature observes strict harmony. The upward ascent in consciousness helps transformation in the lower vehicle, there being a thread of connection between the apex of consciousness and the sub-conscious and the inconscient. A continuous stream of inspiration can pass through this path and can make the lower vehicle luminous in order that consciousness may find its expression there. This task lies before the occultist who is able to establish a direct link between the central being and the sub-liminal and the supraliminal extremes.

Spiritual Discipline

The spiritual discipline in Tantras is essentially a discipline of our central being which has realized consciousness from its limitation. But this discipline is not essentially philosophic or logic or analytic. It is ratner psychic, because it discovers the truth through the direct reading of the life-forces, through their finer modulations and activity and through the acquaintance with the unconscious. Our life-force is connected with the central being. The creation of an individuality between them resists the continuous stream of light and force from the central being. The Tantric discipline removes this creative individuality and directly connects it with the central being and cosmic consciosness.

The psychological discipline in Tantras is different from the spiritual disciplne in the Sāṁkhya and the Vedānta. It unfolds the concrete being in its different sheaths, and traces out the immanent consciousness. The art of the Tantras has been essentially to know the higher range of the spirit and to modulate our being in a way that can give the blessed radiance from the animal vital impulses, and may vibrate the basic urge of the spirit.

In the tradition of *yoga*, the three subtle passages are commonly known as *Iḍā*, *Piṅgalā* and *Suṣumnā*. *Iḍā* is connected with the nasal passage on the left, the *Piṅgalā* is connected with the right. They can be felt under pressure of inhalation and exhalation. *Iḍā* is active when the inhalation or exhalation gets clear inlet or outlet through the left nostril while the *Piṅgalā* is active when the inhalation or exhalation gets easier passage through the right nostril. The *Suṣumnā* is really a subtle luminous path that opens into the vaster spiritual space at top of the brain and connects us directly with the cosmic depths of existence.

Spiritual Realization

The Vedānta primarily indicates discipline in self-realization. Its greatest achievement is the knowledge of the self. Spiritual illumination spreads its radiance. By its affiliating power, it captivates and attracts.

The Vedāntic adepts are more for self-liberation than for establishing a reign of spirituality and a spiritual hegemony. Its passion is to pass into ineffable light, whereas the Tantras give importance to the ideal of spiritualization of the society by infusing spiritual power and light into the constituent members This collective spirituality is the main ideal in the Tantras.

Spiritual Experience

The Tantras accept the process of ascent which reveals the cosmic powers and the wide reach of immediate experiences following them. The Tantras present a wide field of spiritual realization. They provide a spiritual tuning of the being. Every stage of experience brings a new wave of blissful feeling, everyone moving to the higher rhythms of consciousness and higher expressions of being. These experiences are concrete, having definite meaning and expression, as they allow the freedom from the earthly setting of life, and the acquaintance they establish with the spiritual setting. The spiritual aspiration is expressed in difinite ways at the different ladders of the being, and the realization becomes concrete at certain stage of spiritual unfoldment. The spiritual experiences are so removed from the ordinary expereince and they are so subtle that the definite spiritual attitude cannot be mastered unless our being is perfectly responsive.

Cosmic Powers

The direct contact is established with the comic

consciousness and in place of egocentricity, a cosmic-centricity is actually felt. To get access to this unversal centre of consciousness is the ultimate end of the *Kuṇḍalinī Yoga*.

The spiritual life is more than the life of understanding, for it has to deal with the unfolding of our being and with the realization of the divinity that is potential in us. At some stage, the divine power becomes active and helps the spiritualization of our being. The Tantras take the help of the cosmic powers and the cosmic harmonies to make our consciousness active in its subtle expression. The cosmic powers are the expressions of the universal spirit in its definite functioning. They are not actually the expressions of the universal life-force.

Spirit-force is original, while life-force is the imperfect expression of it. The cosmic forces are the spirit-forces in their cosmic manifestations and cosmic functions. They are cosmic emanations; they are over-mental god-heads. They have luminous forms emitting ethereal vibrations and inspiring quick movements and wide comprehensions. They are real cosmic existences, reproductions of the primal power casting light on the progress to the spiritual path.

Śabda-Brahma

Para Bindu or *Śabda-Brahma*, the undiversified infinite conscious energy, out of whom evolves the diversified world of subjects and objects, appears in the individual body as *Kuṇḍalinī Śakti* (conscious spiral energy). She is the conscious creative energy, the Mother of all things that constitute the individual, the world of *Śabda* and *Artha* in him. *Śabda* is the vibration which gradually becomes language, and ultimately, issues out of the vocal organs as articulate sound. An *Artha* is the conceptual counterpart of a *Śabda* which has first a mental shape or though-form, and ultimately, it assumes the form of an object perceptible to any of the senses or the mind.

This world of interacting systems of vibration and resonance in the Tantra Cult accords well with that of the mathematical sciences, as a Tāntrika views his world with an acceptance of all human feelings as interwoven. To live continuously aware of the entire interfused strecture of Reality is the Tāntric bliss. It is this awareness that 'I am Brahman' is liberation, and not the uninspired ritual and any amount of abstract reflection.

Śri Puram is the abode of *Ādi Parā Śakti*. According to Rudrayāmala, which consists of about 1,25,000 ślokas (of which only a few are available now). *Śri Puram* is located beyond all the *lokas* (regions), even beyond *Deva*, *Satya* and *Vaikuṇṭha lokas*. The significance of locating it, even beyond *Vaikuṇṭha lokas*, is that *Śri Mahā Śakti*, taking her abode in the supreme *loka,* is controlling all the manifested and conceptualised universes, performing the three functions of creation, protection and destruction.

The form of *Śri Chakra Yantra* is prescribed in the Tantra Śāstra. The significance attached to this *yantra* is that this *chakra* consists of dots, straight lines and circles. It is well known that the property of matter, if geometrically represented, begins wth a point and proceeds through straight lines or combination of straight lines, and lies triangled or quadrangles or in circles. Therefore, it is the representation of the entire manifested universe that is represented in the *Śri Chakra Yantra*.

The proper way of worship of *Śri Chakra Yantra* is that it should be a three-dimensional *yantra*, with length, breadth and height, because every *yantra* is supposed to be a moving force. In some homes, such a *yantra* is worshipped. In absence of such three-dimensional *yantras,* it is permissible to have a two-dimensional *yantra*, i.e, with width and length drawn in small copper or *pañchloha* metal plates and offer *abhiṣekam* (enthrone) and *pūjā* (worship) to it, meditating upcn it as a three-dimansional *yantra*, i.e., the heigth, which is not there, must be brought up in mental vision through meditation and then worship should be commenced. While so envisioning the heigth, one should call to mind that there are nine tiers of *chakra*. Each tier is known as an *āvaraṇa* (veiling). These nine *āvaraṇas* are together called *Nava-varaṇa*.

The first *chakra* is called *Trilokya Mohana Chakra*. The next one is *Sarvasa Paripūraka Chakra*. This is the second *āvaraṇa*, The third *āvaraṇa* is known as *Sarva Sankhepana Chakra*. The fourth *āvaraṇa,* which is known as *Sarva Soubhāgya Dāyaka Chakra*, is the most important one, and special significance is attached to the *pūjā* of this *āvaraṇa*. The fifth *āvaraṇa* is known as *Sarvaratha Sādhaka Yantra*. The sixth, the seventh and the eighth are respectively *Sarvarakṣakara*, *Sarvarogahāra* and *Sarva Siddhimaya Chakras*. The last one is the *bindu* known as *Sarvanandamaya Chakra*. It is in this *bindu* that *Mahā Śakti* has taken her abode.

Before commencing a *Śri Chakra pūjā* it is necessary to have an initiation in *Śri Vidyā mantra* through a *Guru*. *Pūjā* may be done in accordance with the '*Mantra Upadeśa*' and *Lalita Triśati*, and *Lalita Sahasranāma* may be recited. There is also a *Śri Chakra Aṣṭottari* composed by *Śri Bhāgavadpada*. Those who are initiated in *Pañchadaśākṣari* should recite that *mantra*. Others may recite *Lalita Sahasranāma*, offering *bilva* leaves, *tulsi* or lotus for each name. If *pūjā* cannot be performed for some reason or other, the *Sahasranāma* can be recited as a stotra. Those, who have no time even for this, may offer flowers by uttering only the first and the last name in the *Sahasranāma*, namely *Śri Mātā* and *Śri Lalitāmbikā*.

Liṅga and Yoni

The worship of *liṅga* and *yoni*, i.e., the male and female organs, who also an erortic rite of fertility, the former symbolizing the act of cultivation, and the latter the fruit-bearing earth. Various phallic symobols representing the goddess and her consort have been found during the prehistoric age of India. In Mohenjo-daro also the models of *liṅga* and *yoni* were found, which were perhaps used as life-bestowing amulets, while at Harappa, a number of conical *liṅgas* representing the male organ, and large undulating rings of stones were noticed, which perhaps symbolizes the female principle. Thus the origin of the yoni cult of the later Tantras is found in the pre-historic ruins of Harappa and Mohenjo-daro.

The Tāntric *Śri Chakra* is actually the representation of the female generative organ. The word 'tantra' is derived from the root *tan*, which means 'to spread' or 'to multiply'. The original purpose of the Tāntric rituals was to increase productivity, both natural and human. At the beginning, the male and female organs were worshipped as symbols of procreation and fruitfulness. The *liṅga* was the symbol of the acts of cultivation, while the *yoni* represented the Mother Earth. In later years, the principles of *liṅga* and *yoni* came to be interpreted in terms of a dualistic philosophical outlook.

Mother-right in Tantra

An important feature of the Tantras is the higher standard, to which they raised womanhood.

The ritualistic background of the philosophical Sāṁkhya system was perhaps a form of primitive Tāntricism. The philosphical Sāṁkhya system is essentially the doctrine of *pradhāna* or *prākṛti*, where the status of the *puruṣa* is in a anomalous position in a matriarchal society. Śakti proclaims that She is manifested more in women than in men. In the

Devībhāgavada, certain passages reveal women as the manifestation of the great world cause.

Among the followers of the Tantra school, female shamanesses called *Bhairavis* and *Yoginis* occupy an important place. The seven *padmas* (lotuses) on the *suṣumnā chakra* are the seven seats of feminity inherent in every human being, and *śaktis* like Kulakuṇḍalinī, Vāruṇi, Lakṣmī etc., residing in the lotuses are also conceived as female.

The Acharaneda Tantra prescribes that the *Parā Śakti* should be worshipped only becoming a woman. It seems, therefore, that the Tāntric mode of worship was originally followed by women.

CHAPTER- XX

Conclusion

The path of ascent varied. There is the path to regulate our will, to regulate our intellect and to regulate our emotion. Emphasis sometimes is laid upon working out and developing a particular faculty, something to sharpen all of them, and at the same time to work harmoniously with them. Besides this, there are external and artificial methods to wake up some forms of psychism either through meditation on finer sound currents or light symbols. Vaiṣṇavism has discovered easier paths for spiritual unfolding. It is to open the central being to God in Love and surrender. It is not a passive surrender. It is dynamic and active surrender with spiritual aspiration. It invites the divine power to pour its chastening influence into our being and makes us fit for the eventual realisation. The aspiration makes the whole being of man centred in and receptive of God, and under the divine protecting the seeker can successfully fight against the disturbing forces, inherent in his nature. Every part surrendered becomes transformed by the successful elimination of earth-drawn nature and by the gradual assimilation of the helpful divine assistence. Tāntricism speaks of the intervention of the fine psychic forces towards the final realisation. Vaiṣṇavism is aware of psychic powers and ventures, but it does not make much use of them. It insists more upon the divine inspiration than upon the play of psychic forces. They may install us in power but may ultimately defeat the end.

Vaiṣṇavism starts with the spiritualisation of being under the direct divine guidance. It seeks the conversion of the central being by self-offering and Love. Vaiṣṇavism is insistent upon the union in Love with God and, therefore, leaves aside all the psychic fruition that may come in the way—the possibility of knowledge and power. These achievements are regarded as obstruction to the final achievement in Love. The chief aim is to fill up every inch of our being with aspiration for love and to make it clean, transparent, pure and luminous, so that the divine currents can reach and saturate the whole being. Love is the most powerful of the indrawn forces. It touches the divine direct and makes the divine force active and effective in us. Vaiṣṇavism does not indulge merely in a synoptic vision of reality—it is a secondary cncern, and is the indirect result of the unfolding of our being in love. The actual realisation is profounder, for it is really making the whole forces move and act in divine inspiration, and in enthusiasm for the divine.

Vaiṣṇavism indicates spiritual advance in two ways :—

(1) By more intensive and extensive movement of life in its terrestial expression. (2) And by the impress of spiritual currents on the soul. It believes that finer currents of the soul correspond with the cosmic currents and the progress is indicated by their active expression. In the divine government of the world the adept cannot interfere with God's will, but can be an effective instrument to give a terrestrial expression to it by the affiliation of its will to the divine will. Sacrifice of the individual will is necessary to invite the divine will in its terrestrial expression.

A direct connexion is established and the human will rises from its limitations and functions under divine guidance and inspiration. With this naturally the divine becomes active in man, and he shows incalculable powers and development, because he comes into touch with the creative formations that are underlying the management of the world. But such secrets are never revealed to those who entertain personal motives and it is dangerous to tread in this path unless the total self is sacrified at the divine altar. Divine life and divine power instantaneously come to our help, if there is the offering of our complete being.

God works out His purpose in the different cyclic expression of life, and the mystics are at times the helpmates of God for the realisation of this purpose. They have the divine will working in them. There are occasions when the divine will becomes active in human history.

Even if our will is moved by the divine will, still it has to meet opposition and tension, for the terrestrial evolution is to face inertia of matter. In the working of the divine will, therefore, time is a necessary factor for its effective expression. Strain, tension must play their part in cosmic affairs, and it appears that divine will is defeated at times by them and higher evolution suffers; but the course of evolution is helped by the timely imposition of the divine will and its influence. The course of history makes a sudden change whenever there is such an intervention and new epochs in civilisation are started. Of course the limited vision of man cannot see properly read in philosophic detachment, the manifestation of power, will, wisdom in the inauguration of a new order. For man is always accustomed to understand things in the habitual ways and slow to see the working of new forces. But the working of the divine will in the immanent order is occasional. It does not interfere with the natural order of evolution unless the forces require a re-adjustment or the time in the course of evolution is ripe for an emergence of a new order. Of course the terrestrial forces also become helpful for such an event, they fashion themselves in a way which can make such an event possible. They require re-adjustment, for ultimately nature shows an order, discipline through all its discord and confusion. This is really what in science is called a new emergence—a higher order of existence out of the confusion and the complexities of the lower orders. It requires a strain of imagination to accept the emergence as a blind necessity out of the conflict. The conflict is indicative of the intervention of the divine Will, and the creation of a new epochal history.

The creative order is in a sense a moral order, it is a creative expression in eternal values of justice, righteousness; but still it is an order which has its limitation, for it has to work against the contrary forces of injustice, and unrighteousness. Vaiṣṇavism conceives these values as confined, to the relative order; and they are operative so long as the sense of a spiritual personality in conscious fellowship with the divine has not dawned upon us. Creativity finds its finest expression in the person and only in the order of persons. It can establish a society which is its ultimate consummation. Creativity rises to super-natural expression and seeks to establish a spiritual order, in it alone can it get the highest harmony. But its inherent limitation cannot allow it to establish the perfect order of spirits, or a "civitas dei," though its attempt has always been to reflect the divine life in its completeness and integrity here on earth.

If it can be estabished, it will mean a further emergence in human evolution, where man realises his nature as pure spirit. This is the natural goal of human evolution. This has been so long defeated, for the original limitation in creativity—the expression of spirit through matter—still works. The personality in man is shadowed. It suffers in its complete expression. In individuality there is the sense of 'other,' in personality, this is completely dropped. The sense of the "other" is a sense of separation, which negatives or denies spiritual expression. The full spiritual sense cannot develop in normal life for nature creates the sense of "other" and works through its conflicts and antagonism. Hence Vaiṣṇavism implores the aid of Divine Grace, in order that there may be the full blooming of the spiritual personality and the complete loss of individuality. The personality emerges in full height where all earthly clingings are removed.

There is nothing here which implies effort and tension, nothing which implies a distant goal to be reached. The contraries drop. Life is revealed in Love in its spontaneity. The philosophic effort is replaced by mystic ease. Reason is superseded by intuition. Beauty, Truth and Holiness are simultaneously expressed. This easeness is manifested in *Vaikuṇṭha, i.e.*, that which is freed from all conflicts and contraries—even the contraries of reason.

The expression of divine life in nature is limited by the sense of 'the other.' But here, there is no restriction, for there is no 'other.' It is all spirit. The Vaiṣṇavas characterise this as the order of bliss (*'Hlādinī'* that which is pure Bliss and which gives pure Bliss).The earth is the vale of soul-making. *Vaikuṇṭha* is the vale of self-fulfilment. Even in mystic ascent the opposites meet. At this height all opposition melts away.

Bibliography

Abhinavagupta — *Tantrasāra,* Kashmir Sanskrit Texts and Studies, 17, Srinagar, 1918.

Arthur, E. — *Introduction to Tantra Śāstra,* Ganesh and Company, Madras, 1963.

Arthur, E. — *Śakti and Śākta,* IInd edn., Ganesh and Company, Madras.

Arthur, E. — *Kāmakalā Vilāsa,* Ganesh and Company, Madras, 1963.

Arthur, E. — *Him to Kāli,* Ganesh and Company, Madras, 1965.

Bose, D.N. and Haldhar, H.L. — *Tantras—Their Philosophy and Occult Secrets,* Oriental Publishing House, Calcutta, 1956.

Bhattacharya, B. — *Shakti Sangam—Tantra,* Gaikwad Oriental Series, III pts., Baroda, 1932, 1941, 1947.

Bhattacharya, V. — *Guhya-samāj-tantra,* Gaikwad Oriental Series, Baroda, 1931.

Bhattacharya, V. — *Sādhanāmālā,* 2 parts, Gaikwad Oriental Series, Baroda, 1925-28.

Bharati, A. — *Tantric Tradition,* Raider and Company, London, 1965.

Chakravarti, C. — *The Tantras—Studies on their Religion and Literature,* Punthi Pustak, Calcutta, 1963.

Chaudhury, B. — *Śakti Sādhanā,* Choukhamba Sanskrit Series, Varanasi, 1963.

Duglus, Nick — *Tantra Yoga,* Munshiram Manoharlal, New Delhi, 1971.

Durga Prasad — *Kālivilāsatantra,* Choukhamba Sanskrit Series, Varanasi, 1963.

Ghildiyal, D.P. — *Pañcamakāra Tathā Bhāvatraya,* Kalyan Mandir, Prayag, Samvat 2031.

Gordon, A.K. — *The Iconography of Tibetan Lamaism,* Oxford Publishing Company, New Delhi, 1959.

Guenthur, H.B. — *Yuganaddha—The Tantric View of Life,* Chowkhamba Sanskrit Series, Varanasi, 1964.

Kaviraj, Gopinath — *Yogini Hṛdayam,* Sarasvati Granthamala, ed. 7, Varanasi.

Kaviraj, Gopinath — *Tripura Rahasyam,* Sarasvati Granthamala, ed. 7, Varanasi, 1965.

Kaviraj, Gopinath — *Bharatiya Samskṛti Aur Sādhanā,* Bihar Rashtrabhasha Parisad, Patna, 1963.

Mookerji, A. — *Tantra Āsana,* New Delhi, 1971.

Mookerji, A. — *Yoga Art,* Thams and Hudson, London, 1971.

Mookerji, A. — *Tantra Art,* Kumar Gallery, New Delhi, 1966.

Mishra, J. — *Bhāratīya Pradīka Vidyā,* Bihar Rashtrabhasha Parishad, Patna, 1959.

Mishra, K.L. — *Yogini Tantra,* Gangavishnu, Shrikrishandas, Kalyan, Bombay, 1957.

Narayan — *Tantra-Sāra-Saṁgraha,* Chowkhamba, Sanskrit Series, Varanasi, 1963.

Purnanand — *Śyāmārahasya,* P.C. Paul and Brothers, Calcutta, 1948.

Rauson, Phillip — *The Art of Tantra,* Vikas Publishing House, Delhi, 1973.

Rao, T.A. Gopinath *Elements of Hindu Iconography,* Part 2, (4 parts), Madras, 1914-16.

Shastri, T. Ganapati *Mantramahārṇava,* Sri Lakshmivenkateshvara Steam Press, Kalyana, Bombay, 1940.

Shastri, T. Ganapati *Mantra Siddhi kā Upāya,* Chowkhamba Sanskrit Series, Varanasi, 1963.

Shastri, T. Ganapati *Mātṛkābheda-Tantra,* Chowkhamba Sanskrit Series, Varanasi, 1963.

Shastri, Devadatta *Tantra Siddhānta Aur Sādhana,* Smriti Prakashan, Allahabad, 1976.

Shastri, M.K. *Mālinī Vijyottara Tantra,* Kashmir Sanskrit Texts and Studies, Srinagar, 1922.

Shastri, M.K. *Mṛgendra Tantra,* Kashmir Sanskrit Texts and Studies, edn. 50, Srinagar, 1930.

Shastri, M.K. *Netratantram,* Kashmir Sanskrit Texts and Studies, Srinagar, 1939.

Shastri, R.N. *Mārūtantra,* Sri Lakshmivenkateshvara Steam Press, Kalyana, Bombay, 1940.

Shastri, H.P. *Advayavajra-Saṁgraha,* Gaikwad Oriental Series, edn. 40, Baroda, 1927.

Sarasvati, A.K. *Tantrayan Art,* The Asiatic Society, Calcutta, 1977.

Singh, L.P. *Tantra,* Ananda Nagar, Delhi, 1976.

Snellgrove, D.L. *The Hevajratantra,* IInd Pt., London Oriental Series, Oxford University Press, London, 1959.

Swami, H.S. *Ṣaṭcakra-Nirūpaṇa,* Vijnanapress, Rishikesh, Dehradun, 1973.

Index

Sapta Chakras in the Subtle Body
(Kangra Style, 19th century)

Trinayani (Three-eyed Goddess)
(Stone-Carved Image of Durga, 17th century)

Devī Caṇḍikā
(Ancient form of Goddess Durga)

Tāntric Goddess Shakti
(Post-Vedic Age)

Om-Hrīm Yantra
(The combined seed-syllable of the Universe, containing *Devata* principle)

Śrī Yantra
(A diagrammatic embodiment of the creative sexual activity of the Universe)

Kali Yantra
(The downward-pointing triangle is a female *Yoni*-emblem)

Bhuvaneśwari Yantra
(The *Mahāvidyā* seated in the central triangle)

Viśuddha Chakra

Ājñā Chakra

Sahasrāra Chakra

Chinnamastā
(Rajasthani Image, 18th century)

Mūlādhāra Chakra

Svādhiṣṭhāna Chakra

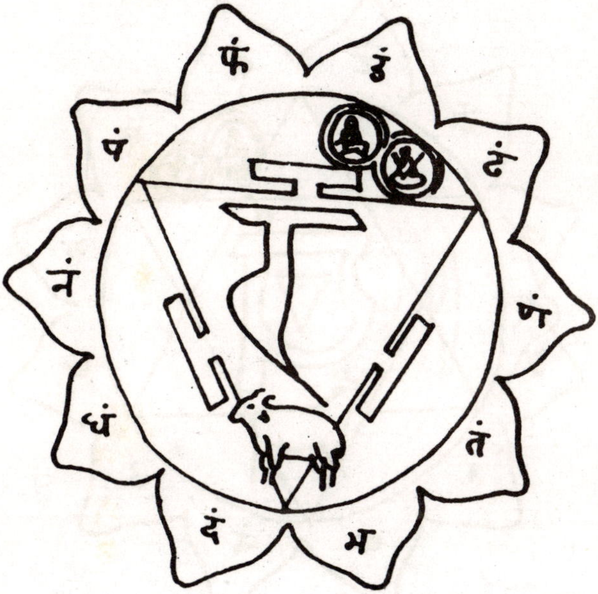

Maṇipūra Chakra

Anāhata Chakra